Adam Joshua Wuthnow
13305 W Dutch Ave
Moundridge, KS 67107

WELCOME TO

HIGH SCHOOL

D0094545

Campus Life Books

After You Graduate
Against All Odds: True Stories of People Who Never Gave Up
Alive: Daily Devotions
Alive 2: Daily Devotions
The Campus Life Guide to Dating
The Campus Life Guide to Making and Keeping Friends
The Campus Life Guide to Surviving High School
Do You Sometimes Feel Like a Nobody?
Life at McPherson High
The Life of the Party: A True Story of Teenage Alcoholism
The Lighter Side of Campus Life
A Love Story: Questions and Answers on Sex
Making Life Make Sense
Peer Pressure: Making It Work for You
Personal Best: A Campus Life Guide
     to Knowing and Liking Yourself
Welcome to High School
What Teenagers Are Saying about Drugs and Alcohol
Worth the Wait: Love, Sex, and Keeping the Dream Alive
You Call This a Family? Making Yours Better

WELCOME TO HIGH SCHOOL

Diane Eble, Chris Lutes & Kris Bearss

A DIVISION OF CTi
CampusLife BOOKS / ZondervanPublishingHouse
Grand Rapids, Michigan

A Division of HarperCollins*Publishers*

Welcome to High School
Copyright © 1991 by Campus Life Books, a division of CTi
All rights reserved

Requests for information should be addressed to:
Zondervan Publishing House
Grand Rapids, Michigan 49530

Library of Congress Cataloging-in-Publication Data

Eble, Diane.
    Welcome to high school / Diane Eble, Chris Lutes, Kris Bearss.
        p. cm.
    "Campus life books."
    ISBN 0-310-71151-7
    1. High school students—United States—Social conditions.
    2. Education, Secondary—United States—Social aspects. I. Lutes,
Chris. II. Bearss, Kris III. Title.
    LC208.4.E25   1991
    373.18'0973—dc20   90-24848
                                            CIP

Designed by Ann Cherryman

Printed in the United States of America

    92   93   94   95   96 / CH / 10 9 8 7 6 5 4 3

CONTENTS

ABOUT THE YOUTHSOURCE™ PUBLISHING GROUP

YOUTHSOURCE™ books, tapes, videos, and other resources pool the expertise of three of the finest youth-ministry resource providers in the world:

Campus Life Books—publishers of the award-winning *Campus Life* magazine, for nearly fifty years helping high schoolers live Christian lives.

Youth Specialties—serving ministers to middle-school, junior-high, and high-school youth for over twenty years through books, magazines, and training events such as the National Youth Workers Convention.

Zondervan Publishing House—one of the oldest, largest, and most respected evangelical Christian publishers in the world.

Campus Life	**Youth Specialties**	**Zondervan**
465 Gundersen Dr.	1224 Greenfield Dr.	1415 Lake Dr., S.E.
Carol Stream, IL 60188	El Cajon, CA 92021	Grand Rapids, MI 49506
708/260-6200	619/440-2333	616/698-6900

INTRODUCTION

What? Welcome to high school? No one's rolling out the welcome mat at all! In fact, suddenly you feel like a little fish in a very big sea of not-necessarily-friendly bigger fish. (You've heard what seniors do to freshmen.) You have lots of fears. You're no longer in the same classes with all the friends you knew and maybe grew up with.

You know high school will be different from junior high.

This is the Big Time.

It's also a confusing time. You're aware that everyone expects so much of you—teachers, parents, friends. It's like there are all these Voices out there, telling you what to do—or what not to do. What to think, who to be.

First, the Voices of Authority—parents, teachers, church leaders. Then the Voices of Friends. The Voices of other influences, like the media. And the voices that come from inside you—from your own feelings, thoughts and desires, as well as the inner voice of your conscience.

Sometimes it gets tiring trying to figure out who to listen to.

But cheer up. Many people have gone before you and survived high school—even thrived. And you're holding in your hand a guide that will help you find a comfortable balance between all these voices.

In fact, that's not a bad way to think of your goal: a balanced life. Picture a pie, divided into four sections, with a smaller circle in the middle. There's the social aspect—how you relate to friends, the opposite sex, family. There's the physical side—feeling comfortable with your body, and making wise choices about what you do with and to it. Then there's the roller-coaster side called feelings.

The intellectual or mental side of you will be challenged with all the new demands of high school, both in class and out. And finally, the spiritual aspect—which, in a balanced life, is really at the center of all the other pieces of the pie, keeping them in harmony.

Each of these aspects—social, emotional, physical, mental, and spiritual—is important. And each aspect will be challenged in new ways in high school. This book addresses each of these challenges in very *practical* detail. It's meant to prepare you to face the worst—and the best—of life in the Big Time.

SECTION 1.

Standing Alone and Finding Friendship

JIM WHITMER

Peer Pressure, Good and Bad

▶ Wolves, Nicole thought as she watched a group of eight guys and girls mercilessly making fun of a short guy with thick glasses. They're just like wolves, tearing people apart not with teeth, but with words.

Nicole knew about wolves. Her friend, Missy, had so wanted to fit in with the pack that she chose to do anything they asked. The wolves didn't think Nicole was cool enough for them, so Missy had snubbed her.

▶ Ever since he could remember, Dan had been shy. In junior high, he'd managed to make a few friends. But now his old friends weren't in any of his classes. He'd have to make new friends or die of loneliness. But how?

▶ Jennifer didn't know where to turn. She felt bad, giving in again to drinking at the party. She knew she shouldn't even have gone, but all her friends were there and she just didn't know how to say no. She thought of talking to her sister Sue about it, but realized that she had been shutting Sue out of her life these days.

She hadn't meant to, but she was just so busy with her new friends and all.

▶ "Hey, Todd, how was your date last night? Did you, you know, do it with her?" Four guys from Todd's gym class waited expectantly for Todd's answer.

"Hey, it's none of your business," Todd said.

"Oooh, that means no, right? How long have you been going out now, three months? Come on, we hear she's put out for other guys. What's wrong with you? I know, you're gay. No . . . you're just scared, right? You don't watch out, you're gonna die the last American virgin."

High school is full of pressures like those Nicole, Dan, Jennifer, and Todd faced. It's a new world, and a bigger world, than you've been in before. There are new pressures, new freedoms, new temptations. Most of them come through people. One of the first things you have to figure out in high school is: how are you going to relate to other people? Where will you find your social niche? And how will it affect you?

The social scene is not all bad, by any means. Plenty of people do make friends, figure out the dating scene, steer a path around the pressure, and have the time of their lives.

Just as pressures and problems come through people, so does the help you need. Let's start there: what kind of friendships do you need? What kind don't you need?

Friends Influencing Friends

When he started junior high, Randy felt lost and alone until he found a special group of friends. Yet there were problems. His new friends got their kicks out of putting others down. At first Randy didn't like teasing and picking fights with "outsiders." But he did feel right about his new friendships. After all, they were the ones who accepted him and gave him a sense of belonging. It wasn't long before Randy was taking part in the put-downs, and enjoying it.

By the time he entered high school, Randy had become a strong and respected leader in his group—a group that was now doing more than just picking on others. Regularly, Randy and his friends met in the park behind the school to smoke marijuana and drink beer. They also started vandalizing the school. Needless to say, Randy's group gained a very bad reputation.

Yet this story has a good ending. A few months into his freshman year, Randy began to see the importance of making his own decisions, apart from the group. He also grew tired of getting into trouble. So he chose to take advantage of some of the new friend-making opportunities high school offered. He met some Christian kids and even became involved in a local church youth group. Although Randy had started high school on very shaky ground, he eventually changed his behavior and his reputation—for good. As a natural leader, Randy also became a positive influence on many others.

Your junior-high experience may have been quite different from Randy's. But like Randy, your freshman year will undoubtedly offer many new friendship opportunities. Choose wisely. The decisions you make now will undoubtedly affect you throughout the rest of high school.

How to Avoid Negative Friendship Pressure

Here are guidelines to help you better understand and deal with negative friendship pressure:

▶ Realize that everybody is influenced by friendship pressure. It's not a crime to admit that you're influenced by others, nor is the influence necessarily bad. For example, it's not wrong to wear a certain type of gym shoe or designer clothing because others do. It's only natural to want to fit in. But by admitting that friendship pressure does influence you, you'll be better able to recognize and deal with those influences that are clearly wrong.

▶ Decide right now what you will and won't do. What are your values? What do you believe is right and wrong for you—not for the group? Do this: Make a list of things you will and won't do. For instance: I will only go to parties where adults are present. I will look for friends who believe drug abuse and drinking are wrong. I won't use language I feel is offensive. I won't watch R-rated videos. I won't cheat on tests. I won't participate in excluding or putting down outsiders. Refer to this list often, especially when you are tempted by negative friendship pressure.

▶ Seek friends who are a positive influence. As you consider new friendships, look for people who will have a good influence on your life, your personal beliefs, and your values.

▶ Avoid putting negative friendship pressure on others. For example: It's OK to wear your hair a certain way; it's not OK to reject others who don't wear their hair that way. This holds true for all kinds of behavior. By accepting people for who they are, you can help relieve friendship pressure others face.

How to Use Positive Friendship Pressure

Friendship pressure isn't all bad. In fact, you and your friends can have a very positive influence on your school. Here's how:

▶ Set the pace. As an underclassman, you feel like you have no power in your school. Probably every underclassman feels that way. Yet what if you let other underclassman know you don't like putting others down? Might they think twice before tossing out another putdown? Couldn't you be a force for positive change among your own friends? Further, couldn't your friends be a force for change among their friends? And once positive friendship pressure gets started, who knows where it will stop?

▶ Search for alternatives. Don't just say no to negative influences. Say yes to positives. Here is a challenge: Make a list of all the negative activities that go on among your friends and classmates. Next try to think of a positive alternative for each negative. Write your alternatives out, being as specific and creative as possible. For instance: negative, drinking parties; positive, a non-alcoholic party where everybody dresses like a rock star they can't stand. Share your list with some friends and brainstorm even more ideas. Obviously, your efforts will help you and your friends discover many fun activities. But why not share the list with others outside your group, like your class president? It could help change your entire school.

▶ Join positive clubs or organizations. Most schools have groups like SADD and many have Christian clubs like Student Venture, Campus Life, or Young Life. There are also many schools with peer counseling or peer tutoring programs. Find out what's available and become a positive influence through involvement in a worthwhile club or organization.

▶ Be your own best influence. You will undoubtedly face obstacles as you try to influence others. At times you will undoubtedly fail in your efforts. But you won't be a failure. Your decisions to use positive friendship pressure are influencing at least one person— you. And that's the best possible influence you can have.

Finding New Friends

If you're typical, you feel alone and friendless now that you're in high school. It doesn't seem like you have any of your old friends in your new classes. Or maybe you're simply ready to take advantage of new friendship opportunities. Whatever the case, you know you'd like to make some new friends. But how?

First, think about a few people you would like to meet. Possibly it's the guy whose locker is across the hall. Or maybe it's the girl who sits across from you in English class. Now, think about a few people who would like to meet you. Maybe it's the girl who always eats alone at lunch. Or possibly it's the guy who always waits by himself at the bus stop. Here is the point: Along with seeking friendship with people you'd like to know, reach out to a few people who need a friend like you. As you do, you'll be surprised at how much you receive from even the giving side of friendship.

Friendship Starters

Want to make a new friend, but don't know where to begin? Try these ideas on individuals you'd like to know better:

▶ Be friendly. Say hello. Smile. Show interest in what this person is doing. Assume that everybody you meet will appreciate your interest. You'll be right ninety percent of the time.

▶ Remember names. By remembering a person's name, you've taken an important step toward friendship.

▶ Listen. Make eye contact when someone is talking to you. Ask questions and wait patiently for a response.

▶ Pay attention to the little things. When listening, focus on important details the person says about himself. Next time your paths cross, you can refer back to that earlier conversation. Undoubtedly he'll be impressed that you cared enough to remember what he said.

▶ Say a good word. Everyone likes to be complimented. Do it often.

▶ Laugh. A good sense of humor goes a long way in building a solid friendship.

▶ Respect a person's space. Everybody needs time for themselves and other friends. If you're always waiting at her locker, or always shoving your way behind him in the lunch line, you'll quickly wear out your welcome.

▶ Open up slowly. Initially, stick with talking about everyday stuff (the weather, homework, Friday's game). Those deeper conversations will come naturally as a closer friendship develops.

Too Shy to Make Friends?

Trisha sat silently as others joined in the discussion. Although she was a part of the group, she seemed somehow separate and alone. It was apparent that no one there considered Trisha a close friend.

The adult visitor who led the discussion sensed the girl's shyness and decided to ask her a question. There was a moment of nervous silence as all eyes turned toward Trisha. The visitor waited patiently. Finally Trisha spoke, slowly and softly at first. As the visitor smiled and gave nods of encouragement, she spoke a little more confidently. She offered a few insights that surprised the group, who had become accustomed to her silence. When the discussion ended, Trisha went up to one of the other adults present and said excitedly: "I actually talked!"

Trisha's problem is not uncommon. Many of us have streaks of shyness, especially when it comes to making new friends. Yet shyness need not hold anyone back. Even Trisha, with a little encouragement, took a big step forward. And you too can have similar successes, if you're willing try these simple suggestions:

▶ Take safe risks. Practice talking around people who know you well. Get a close friend or family member to ask you questions that will help you open up a little more. The important thing is that you learn to talk comfortably around those you know and trust. In doing so, you will be better prepared to talk to people you'd like to know better.

▶ Speak when spoken to. When that sophomore on the bus says, "How's it going?"—smile and offer an answer. Even if your answer is brief, you have shown your willingness to talk.

▶ Begin conversations that have natural time limits. Think about those few moments before the bell rings or before a teacher calls the class to order. Use that time to start brief conversations. Doing this will assure you that the conversation won't go on forever. It will also demonstrate your desire to be friendly and open.

▶ Join activities that don't require a lot of talking. Get involved in team sports, clubs, a church youth group—any group where you can simply be around other people. Doing this will help you feel more comfortable around others and could certainly lead to some very natural friendship opportunities.

▶ Learn to like yourself for who you are. There is nothing wrong with being shy. Such an admission can go a long way in helping you be at ease with yourself. When you begin to feel more comfortable around yourself, you'll naturally feel more comfortable around other people.

Keeping Friendship Alive

A group of high-school students gathered to talk about friendship. Despite their many differences of opinion, they all agreed: Good friends are trusting, loyal, and honest. Good friends, they said over and over, don't back-stab or repeat something said in confidence. Good friends, they stressed, are there when you need them and stand by you during the hardest of times.

These insights should be taken seriously by all who are serious about friendship. Traits like loyalty, honesty, truthfulness, trustworthiness, and faithfulness are not simply nice virtues. They represent the core of what it means to be a true friend. Practice them and you'll be on your way to lasting, solid friendships.

Avoid These Friendship Destroyers

Don't let your friendship be destroyed by any of the following:

▶ Jealousy. Don't be envious, but celebrate together your friend's achievements and good fortunes.

▶ Gossip. Hearsay, secrets made public, half-truths told—they're guaranteed to kill a friendship.

▶ Disloyalty. True friends stick by you, and never stick a verbal knife in your back.

▶ Competition. Friendship is not a contest you're always trying to win. It's a team sport where you cheer each other on.

▶ Negativism. A constant bad attitude is a good way to lose a friend.

▶ Comparison. Never compare a friend to anyone else. Instead, appreciate and praise your friend for the unique skills and qualities he has.

▶ Selfishness. A friend who is concerned only about herself is not really concerned about friendship.

▶ Possessiveness. Hang on too tightly and you'll suffocate your friendship.

When Problems Enter a Friendship

Your own experience tells you that friendships are not trouble-free. Yet serious problems like jealousy, gossip and lying need not rip a friendship apart. In fact, most "friendships tears" can be mended. Here's how:

▶ Confrontation. You and your friend must deal with serious problems immediately and tactfully. Don't let those problems eat away at your friendship. But when you do let your friend know what's bothering you, don't use harsh language, and avoid putting all the blame on the other person. More than likely you share some of the guilt too.

And always, before confronting, ask yourself: Is this really worth bringing up? Sometimes we mistake personality differences and differences in lifestyle for real problems. Fingernail biting, weird laughs, a love for loud music, and an occasional belch at the table are far from major concerns. Learn to crack good-natured jokes about this kind of stuff. Agree to disagree. But don't put such behavior on the same level as real problems. After all, you expect your friend to accept your personal quirks. Doesn't he deserve the same courtesy?

▶ Forgiveness. Learn to say, "I'm sorry." Obviously, friendships aren't perfect. Both you and your friend will have plenty of opportunities to give and seek forgiveness. While it's not easy, forgiveness is the first and most important step in healing a broken friendship. Conversely, friendship without forgiveness is friendship doomed to fail.

When Friendship Fails

You and your friend have tried but simply can't get along. Or your beliefs and values are so different that you're constantly tempted to go against what you feel is right. Friendships that become more hassle than fun are probably friendships that are ready to be called off. No, don't go away enemies. Yes, still speak to each other when you pass in the halls. But pull away enough so you can gain freedom from a bad situation. Doing so will give you the time and energy to pursue positive, healthier friendships.

How Do I Find Romance?

One of the most exciting things about high school is the potential for forming deeper relationships with the opposite sex. But for many, the question is how to start the romance ball rolling in the first place.

Take Rick, for instance. His problem was shyness around girls—especially girls he felt attracted to. Rick needed a way to conquer his shyness enough to ask someone out.

The Friendship Factor

The answer for Rick was to concentrate on getting to know girls as friends. He concentrated on the friendship skills mentioned earlier, and found that making friends with a variety of people increased his confidence. He visited a couple of other church youth groups and got to know others who shared his values. He also joined a Christian group that met in his school. It's not surprising that Rick found several girls he liked, and eventually he asked Keisha out. Because they had known each other from youth group activities, Rick felt comfortable around Keisha and they had a good relationship for several months. When they broke up, they remained friends.

Making friends with a variety of people is a great way to find romance. Get involved in activities that interest you, and you're bound to meet other people who share the same interest. From there, you get to know one another through the shared activities, and then if there's mutual interest and something to build a relationship on, you let the person know you're interested in a deeper relationship.

But that last step—letting the other person know you're interested—can be difficult. It's difficult for guys to get up the courage to ask someone out. It's difficult for girls to wait for someone to ask them out. Sometimes the only thing to do is take the plunge. Expect some bruises along the way, but know that it's the only way to get started on the sometimes-rocky road to love.

Getting Dates: For Guys

For guys, getting a date is seemingly easy—you just ask a girl out. Easier said than done, right? One way to get over the terror of being rejected is to concentrate on group dating. It can be real casual, basically just a bunch of guys and girls getting together to do something fun. From there, it's not such a big deal to ask one girl out on a casual date—or to double date.

Here's a tip: When you go out, plan to do something that helps you get to know each other. A walk, an athletic event, miniature golf, a movie and burgers or pizza afterward, even doing homework can help you get to know the other person as a person. Making out for hours in the back seat does not help you to get to know someone.

Getting Dates: For Girls

Shelley had a lot of guy friends already. Her problem was that none of them asked her out. How could Shelley let them know her feelings without scaring them away?

The direct approach. Being up-front and direct is often the best way. This doesn't mean telling a person you get hives every time you walk by his locker. That can scare anyone! (If it doesn't, it has a tendency to heat up the relationship prematurely.)

But there's nothing wrong with asking a guy out on a casual date. Few guys nowadays object to that; most are delighted. Just remember to keep your approach casual. Yes, the direct approach is scary. It's scary for guys, too. But it beats sitting around feeling lonely.

Indirect approaches. Maybe the direct approach just isn't your style. Here are some more subtle ways to signal interest:

▶ Sending nonverbal cues: smiling a lot, saying hello and good-bye, and making a lot of eye contact. Singling him out and showing your interest in what he's involved in. This may terrify a shy guy, but it often works.

▶ Sending a message through a mutual friend.

▶ Inviting the guy you're interested in (along with others) to join a group outing, such as a hike or a concert or a fancy you-cook-it dinner.

▶ Sending a card to recognize something special in his life: an athletic or academic achievement, a birthday, or just a special greeting. (But do sign it, or you'll defeat the purpose: to let him know you are interested.)

Avoid These Traps

Dating in high school can seem like a big game in which the rules are never written down, and only a few lucky people seem instinctively to know them. But here are a few tips to help you avoid some of the things that commonly trip people up as they try to make sense out of dating.

▶ Being too desperate. Trying too hard to get someone usually backfires. Think about it: Are you more attracted to someone you know is obsessed with finding a date, or someone who knows how to have fun and get along with people even when "unattached"? The most attractive people are those who are involved with life and other people, not plotting how to snag a date for the next school dance.

▶ Chasing only the most popular people. A lot of the finer people in the world lack the outstanding looks or personality that automatically draws other people to them. But if you take the time to get to know "ordinary people," you'll almost certainly meet some you like. Look for friends, and you may find a special someone.

▶ Dating only for status. Suppose the captain of the football team asks you out. You really don't have much in common—and you've heard he has a reputation for pushing girls to get sexually involved—but how can you say no, when half the girls in the school are dying to go out with him? Or perhaps you're a guy who finds your biology lab partner funny and interesting. Only problem: She's not a knockout, and what would your friends say if you started dating her?

Friendship pressure can influence who you go out with. Give in, and you'll either compromise your values or lose out on some good relationships. Why not spark a little positive friendship pressure by letting people know that you intend to choose relationships for yourself? Those who have done so report that friends almost always end up respecting them.

▶ Letting shyness limit you. Shyness is a big problem for some, and it's OK not to push yourself too hard. But do push yourself in little ways: smile, say hi, ask a question about a homework assignment. Slowly you'll find yourself feeling more comfortable with people. It's worth all the clammy hands and awkwardness to inch your way out of your shyness.

When You Have a Special Someone

Romantic relationships usually follow this pattern: first, star-struck love. Second, flaws in paradise—you realize the person isn't perfect; she has an irritating giggle or he doesn't wash his hair as much as you'd like. Or maybe it's a deeper issue; you realize you really have little in common after all.

At this point, it's decision time: Either you split, or you commit yourself to exploring a deeper love. If love is to last, it must change from something that happens to you—star-struck love—to something you choose.

And how do you know whether you should split or commit?

Think of a healthy relationship as Friendship Plus—friendship plus romance. Romance tends to take care of itself. Work on the friendship side of it—things like mutual respect, consideration, sharing your thoughts and feelings, being honest, having fun. Not to mention patience, kindness, forgiveness, trust, the desire to protect the other from harm, and a lack of envy or boastfulness or rudeness or self-seeking. (Check out 1 Corinthians 13 in the Bible for more details.) Concentrate on these things, and whether or not you find lasting love in high school, you'll have many positive, lasting memories.

TOO SHY TO ASK DARLA OUT IN PERSON,
WAYNE RESORTED TO DRASTIC MEASURES.

When Friends and Romance Are Hard to Come By

It's another Saturday night, and you're home by yourself . . . again. You asked three different friends to come over, but they all had other plans. Even Mom and Dad went out tonight. So what do you do with the quiet, the privacy . . . the aloneness?

One of two things. There's the not-so-good choice of sulking the night away in front of the TV with a bag of chips and a six-pack of Coke, convinced life is rotten and the world is unfair. This is "loneliness"—being alone when you don't want to be.

Or, you can take a better route, and decide to actually make good use of the time. To enjoy having the entire house/stereo/VCR/TV to yourself for a few hours. This is the up side of being alone. It's called "solitude"—being content with being alone.

Solitude you enjoy. Loneliness you won't.

There will be times throughout your life when being alone isn't your first choice. But being alone doesn't hurt until you start to feel lonely. (That's why it's possible to feel lonely even in a crowd of people.)

You can generally avoid loneliness, though, by learning to be good company to yourself.

What's Good about Sometimes Being Alone?

▶ Uninterrupted time to do all the things you've wanted to do but haven't gotten around to.

▶ Perspective. You can sort through your problems and collect your emotions by getting away from the confusion. Alone times also help you make sense out of life by giving you a chance to listen to yourself and God.

▶ A stronger you. You'll discover what motivates you, what you like about yourself, what you need to change. And as you clarify your abilities and your beliefs, you'll learn to more confidently face peer pressure and be a better friend.

▶ Plans. It's your opportunity to set goals, make clear decisions and plan for what's ahead.

▶ Preparing for life. The things you enjoy in your solitude will probably become lifetime interests of yours. And it's possible that the skills you develop now will turn into a career.

Making Alone Times Work for You

Need some ideas for turning alone times into solitude? Try any of these that interest you:
▶ Go for a walk
▶ Compile a tape of your favorite songs
▶ Read for fun
▶ Exercise/lift weights
▶ Do crafts

- Skateboard
- Compose a song or poem
- Build model planes/cars
- Learn a new skill: painting, drawing, sewing
- Write in your journal
- Play with your dog or cat
- Go fishing
- Read the Bible and pray
- See a movie
- Write letters or notes of appreciation to people
- Organize your room/papers/clothes
- Work on engines/motors
- Take up a new instrument such as the guitar

You will become more comfortable with being alone if you'll actually plan an alone time. Make it something you can look forward to. Decide you're going to ride a bike to your favorite spot. Take your journal, pack a lunch, and bring along some good music. Then enjoy an afternoon to yourself.

Or take your favorite hobby to the garage or a faraway room in the house, and work at it for as long as you feel like it. Or get out and exercise, then treat yourself to the frozen yogurt of your choice.

The point is, you can learn how to be alone and enjoy it. And one of the best benefits is that learning how to be alone helps you get past any fear of being alone.

When You've Had Enough Alone Time

After all is said and done, it's important to realize that you always have an option when you start to feel lonely—or when you grow tired of being alone. That option involves getting out of your room and getting with other people.

Even if your closest friends are busy, there are students at school, at church, and next door who could use a friend but who are too shy to step up and introduce themselves. So you do it. Take the initiative and make a new friend. Invite them to your house, plan to meet for burgers, ask if they want to go roller-skating with you.

And there's always one other surefire way to forget your loneliness: Do something to help other people. It not only feels right, but you'll end up feeling better about yourself.

The Trouble with Parents

Mike has his share of complaints about his family. His dad can be very stubborn and terribly strict. His mom tends to "mother" him to death. Then there's his older sister Tracy, a senior in high school. She doesn't seem to have much time for him any more.

Yet Mike doesn't put all the blame on his family. He admits, for instance, that he's pretty jealous of Tracy's friends. He knows he tends to pout when things don't go his way. He also realizes he does some stuff that's pretty irritating, like clipping sports articles from a newspaper nobody else has read.

There is something else Mike is willing to admit: His parents and older sister have many good points. "Even though she's busy," says Mike, "Tracy does try to include me as much as possible." Mike has some good things to say about his father, too, like, "When Dad knows he's been a little too hard on me, he'll come up to my room after I've gone to bed to say he's sorry. I may still be mad at him, but down deep I'm glad he's willing to do that." As for his mother, Mike says that while she's "a little too huggy at times—I know she loves me a lot. She's always there when I have a problem." He also knows that he too brings a lot of pluses to family life, such as a good sense of humor: "Sometimes things get a little too serious, so I start joking around. Doing that helps us all to lighten up a little."

Mike's attitude is a pretty good one. Amid the complaints, he's willing to admit he's sometimes part of the problem. He's also willing to talk about his family's good points. All in all, he's able to see that his home isn't such a bad place to live.

Spend some time thinking about your family. Think about the bad side, including the problems you help create. Then think about all the good each family member has to offer—including what you have to offer. As you look at both the good and the bad of family life, you may, like Mike, gain a more balanced, realistic view of what it means to be a family. You may also realize, like Mike, that you have a few good reasons to be thankful.

Getting Along with Your Parents

Ever think you're in a tug of war with your parents? You're braced at one end of the rope and your mom and dad stand rigid at the other. They're trying to pull you back to childhood. Tug. You're straining hard for more freedom, more independence. Tug. Now that you're in high school, the tug of war seems even more intense. You think you're old enough to make decisions—to be trusted. Tug. They still want to make a lot of decisions for you. In fact, they're scared by what they hear about drugs, drinking, sex in high school. Tug.

Instead of fighting from opposite sides, why not

join the same team? After all, you are family—a team who should want the best for all its members. As you start pulling together, your parents may discover that you're a lot stronger than you used to be. They may even be willing to let go and give you a chance to pull alone for a while—allowing you to make more of your own decisions, giving you a little more responsibility. Of course, they'll still be on the sidelines cheering you on, always ready to lend a hand when needed. And doesn't that sound a lot better than engaging each other in a tug of war?

Talking Through Problems with Your Parents

When you feel treated unfairly or misunderstood, you wonder: What can you do to be heard? Here are a few tips for improving family communication:

▶ Think before you react. Nagging and arguing will only make your parents defensive and all the more convinced they're right. Don't do it. Further, give yourself time to think through why they reached the conclusion they did. Try to understand their side. In doing so, you may discover they have good reasons for thinking the way they do.

▶ Talk only when the time is right. Hot tempers are only waiting to explode. Give both you and your parents a chance to cool off. Get together when everyone is relaxed and ready to hear each other out.

▶ Listen to their side of the story. Let your parents have their say—even if you're sure they're wrong. Listening attentively "communicates" much more than your finest argument. In fact, doing so demonstrates a great deal of personal maturity. Even if they still hold to their original position, they should at least be impressed by your willingness to hear them out.

▶ Present your side in a non-threatening, reasonable manner. Don't yell and don't use words that are accusatory and loaded with emotion. "You never let me do anything!" may be packed with feeling, but certainly won't help your position.

"Give me an N, give me an O. What's that spell? NO! What's that spell? NO!"

▶ Be willing to compromise. Maybe your parents won't let you go out alone with your boyfriend/girlfriend. OK, see if they'll let you meet your special friend at Pizza Hut with a group of friends. When you compromise you won't get everything you want. More often than not, though, you will find a workable solution you and your parents can live with.

▶ Accept the final solution. Arguing, pouting, or going against your parents' decision only makes matters worse. True, their decision may not be what you wanted. It may not even be fair. Yet while you are still in your parents' home, they are ultimately in charge. Fighting their decision will not change that. On the other hand, consider this: As they see your efforts to accept their decision, they may be willing to ease up a little. And in the long run, you may find yourself with more freedom and more choices than you ever thought possible.

How to Gain Your Parents' Trust

You say you want your parents to trust you more? Here are five steps to greater independence:

▶ Show you're trustworthy. Demonstrate you can be trusted and your parents will be ready to hand out more trust.

▶ Be responsible for the little things. A clean room, a chore done cheerfully, homework completed on time—all those little things add up to one big thing: more responsibility. More trust.

▶ Get their advice. You ask for help and they trust you more. Why? Because they know you'll be back when a decision gets too hard to handle.

▶ Communicate your values and beliefs. "I'll do this, but I won't do that." Telling and showing your parents what you will and won't do can only help them trust you more.

▶ Keep in the boundaries. Your parents said you could do this, this and this—but not that. Don't stretch the boundaries or you will find them shrinking.

Advice for Step-families

Here are some tips for those who suddenly find themselves part of a step-family:

▶ Be willing to give and take. No longer is your home "all your own." You now must be willing to share it with a whole new set of people. As hard as it might be, you have to decide personally that you are willing to give and take. An unwillingness to do so simply adds to the stress and tension that is already incredibly high.

▶ Plan family meetings. You and your step-parent and step-siblings came together as "virtual strangers." You need to take extra effort to become a family. That's why regular meetings—where problems, concerns, and rules get discussed—are so important.

▶ You must let go of the past. This doesn't mean that the parent who no longer lives in your house is not a parent. He or she is still a crucial part of your life. And your brothers and sisters who live away will always be your siblings. But you also must come to grips with the fact that things have changed. Admitting this is very hard, yet doing so will allow you to more readily accept your new situation.

▶ Talk through your fears. Obviously you have many fears and frustrations about your new step-family. If you are unable to talk about this at home, find a trusted adult friend who can listen and offer advice. Meet with this friend regularly, not to gossip, but to help you work through the problems created by your new family.

When Your Values Differ

You and your parents obviously have disagreements. Some may never be resolved. You may simply have to "agree to disagree." But what happens when disagreements get in the way of those things you value most? Say they drink, you don't. Or maybe you enjoy church, they'd rather sleep in. What can you do?

▶ Don't condemn their behavior. This will only cause trouble. Sure, you can voice your concern: "Mom, I care about you, and everything I read tells me that smoking is extremely addictive and very harmful to your health." Beyond that, there isn't much you can do or say.

▶ If you do feel your parents want you to do something that is clearly wrong, talk to them about it. (See "Talking Through Problems with Your Parents.") If that doesn't seem to help, seek guidance from a trusted adult friend: a pastor, Christian psychologist, or the counselor at your school.

▶ Stick by the rules that are good for you. Don't complicate matters by disobeying those rules your parents set that are clearly for your own good.

Sometimes, family situations become too hard to handle. When there are serious family disorders—such as alcoholism, drug abuse, physical or sexual abuse, or incest—help must be found right away. Don't go it alone. Get professional assistance immediately.

Riding the Roller Coaster Called Feelings

The Yo-Yo Effect

▶ Jessica woke up on Tuesday feeling great. The sun was shining, she remembered that her best friend had told her Rob liked her, she had just had her hair cut and liked the style. She took a shower and stood in front of her closet trying to decide what to wear.

Then she remembered. There was going to be an algebra quiz today, and she hadn't studied! Panic seized her. To make matters worse, she had nothing to wear. And when she dried her hair, it didn't look at all like it had yesterday when the hair stylist fixed it. Suddenly Jessica felt like her world had gone all wrong and nothing would ever go right again.

▶ Three minutes before the end of the state basketball championship game, Manny fouled out. The ref's call was questionable, and the entire team protested, but Manny was sent to the bench anyway. By the time he reached the sidelines, he was steaming.

"Did you see what they did to me?" Manny hollered at the coach.

"Forget it, Wilson. Sit down and cool off!"

"But Coach, he deliberately—"

"You heard me. Calm down or hit the showers!"

Dealing with Feelings

Feelings. They bring you up, they pull you down, as if you were a yo-yo on a string.

There are times when it's easy to control anger; other times it seems to explode out of nowhere. Depression can seem to come from nowhere and hang on. Or a seemingly insignificant event—your mom returning to full-time work, for instance—somehow triggers strong feelings of anxiety.

It's enough to make you feel slightly crazy. But you're not. The yo-yo effect is just part of growing up. Rest assured, you're normal.

That doesn't mean, however, that it's easy to deal with emotions. Feelings, especially powerful ones like anger or jealousy, can be pretty messy. People get uncomfortable when they watch someone dissolve into tears or turn beet-red with rage. The discomfort prompts them to make comments like "Calm down!" or "Snap out of it!" or "Quit overreacting!" How often has someone told you, in effect, "Control your emotions; put a lid on your feelings"?

But ignoring or avoiding painful feelings won't make them go away. The fact is that, one way or another, strong feelings will always boil to the surface—usually when you least expect them.

You can ignore, deny, or hold in your emotions only so long and then—Blam!—they explode. Often without warning.

Feelings are a special part of life in high school. You'll always have feelings. But during this time of your life, they seem to come out in stronger colors.

The Truth about Feelings

We tend to label feelings "good" or "bad." But the truth is that feelings themselves are neither good nor bad. Feelings are just feelings. They are neutral. How you react to your feelings, however, is not neutral. Your responses can be either positive or negative.

Feelings are really physical responses to powerful thoughts. The mind thinks and the body reacts to the thought. Manny's anger was his body's spontaneous reaction to the powerful thought, I've been treated unfairly! Jessica's anxiety came because she felt threatened by the thought of getting a bad grade on her algebra quiz, and by the thought that if she didn't look just right, Rob might change his mind about her.

Since emotions are merely physical reactions connected with thoughts, there is no way the emotions themselves can be considered good or bad.

Color My World

Still, when feelings are carrying you up and down like a dizzying roller coaster ride, you might be tempted to think life would be easier without emotions. But think of this for a second: Feelings are what color our world and make it interesting. We even speak in terms of "red-hot anger," the "green-eyed monster of jealousy," or "the blues."

God himself has emotions. The Bible speaks of his jealousy, his anger and sorrow at sin, his tender care, his joy. Being made in God's image apparently means being uniquely able to experience emotions.

In this section we'll talk about how to learn to ride the roller coaster and even, perhaps, enjoy the ride.

How to Handle Angry Feelings

"Don't you dare leave this house!" Trisha's mom shouted. Ignoring the warning, Trisha slammed out the back door. Trisha was angry at her parents for treating her like she was still in junior high. She was angry at her brother and sister for always getting their way. She was angry at the bad wind storm that had caused severe damage to her home. She was angry that her parents fought over money all the time. Keeping it buried deep inside, her anger only increased. One day it would no doubt explode on a parent, teacher, or friend. Or maybe it would erupt internally, causing long-lasting emotional scars.

Anger. It can make us bitter, withdrawn, negative. Rarely, but sometimes, it turns us mean, violent, even self-destructive. It can cripple or destroy friendships and other relationships. The fact is, if we don't learn to control our anger—it will control us. The next time you feel angry, here are some things to try:

▶ Breathe deeply. Count to ten (or a hundred). Take a long walk. Just do something to help you calm down.

▶ Go for a run. Doing physical exercise helps relieve tension and anger.

▶ Beat up your pillow. Scream at the walls. Just do something to let some of the anger get out.

▶ Learn to laugh. Serious problems should be taken seriously, but stupid stuff shouldn't. Instead of getting mad, just have a good laugh at life's silly irritations.

▶ Write a nasty letter. Write a letter to the person or people who made you angry. Or your letter could simply be "to" a situation or circumstance that's really bothering you. Write furiously, write honestly. Next step: Rip the letter into a thousand pieces. Doing so will help keep you from ripping into another person—from doing something you'll later regret. Most important, it will help you get some of that anger off your chest.

▶ Shout at God. He can take it. He's seen anger before, he's even experienced it. If you blame him, say so. Just tell him what you're feeling. Then allow him to talk to you: Spend some time reading and thinking about Scripture that addresses anger (Ephesians 4:26, Psalm 4, Colossians 3:8, James 1:19).

▶ Try to discover what made you angry. On the surface, you may be angry at your mother for accidentally tossing away your homework, at your brother for eating your candy bar, at a friend for failing to pick you up. Yet all those things may be symptoms of some deeper hurt, like your parents' divorce, a friend's betrayal, a close relative's untimely death. By pinpointing the source of your anger, you can begin to deal with the real problem.

▶ Confront. After you've blown off some steam, you may still feel you need to confront the person who made you angry. Go ahead. But do it without emotional or accusatory language. Don't tell him what kind of person he is; tell him how you feel. Be firm, but gentle. And if you were part of the problem, admit it.

▶ Forgive others. People full of bitterness and hatred are people who refuse to forgive. So forgive—for your own good.

▶ Forgive yourself. You're only human; you make mistakes. So look at yourself in the mirror and say, "You're forgiven."

▶ Say you're sorry. Don't let emotional outbursts destroy relationships and friendships. If your anger hurt someone, apologize—even if you feel you had good reason to feel angry.

▶ Use good anger to do good. It's good to be mad about environmental pollution. It's good to be mad at kids who drive drunk. It's good to be mad because there are homeless and hungry people. Vent that anger by doing something constructive and positive. For instance, join SADD, spend a summer building homes for the poor, work in a soup kitchen on weekends.

▶ If needed, seek professional help. If your anger causes you to be destructive or violent, continually depressed or totally withdrawn from your family, seek assistance from a professional Christian counselor right away.

Why Am I
So Blue?

In a high-school survey on depression, 100 percent of those who returned the survey said they had been depressed. But only 14 percent of the students thought that other people got depressed, too.

Feeling "down" is perfectly normal, especially during the high-school years. It's the natural response to change, loss and pressure—and there are plenty of these in high school. Your body has already begun to change, your relationships with parents and friends are changing, your mind is changing.

Each change means a loss, a loss of the familiar. And loss makes us feel down, "blue." Even seemingly insignificant losses, like a change in schedule, can trigger the blues. You feel let down, sad, pessimistic, fearful of not being able to live up to expectations (your own, your parents' or your friends'). You don't want to be with people. Or else you fill your life with a flurry of activity, but feel empty inside. You're battling the blues.

Getting Up When You're Feeling Down

While feeling down occasionally is perfectly normal, that doesn't mean you have to stay down. There are some things you can try to make yourself feel better.

► Get some exercise. Strenuous physical activity tends to work off the blues and the blahs, and releases certain "feel-good" chemicals in the brain. Ride your bike, shoot some baskets, put on some music and dance. Don't just sit there, get active!

► Talk to someone. Find someone who will listen as you talk through your feelings. This will help you feel less isolated. Isolation increases your feelings of helplessness and hopelessness.

► Keep a journal or diary. Write down what's bothering you. Don't worry about punctuation or grammar; no one will see this but you.

► Remember the good. Make a list of the things that have been good in your past life, of activities you've enjoyed or been good at in the past, of things you enjoy or are good at today, and activities that you might look forward to. Then, try one of these activities.

► Check out what you're telling yourself. Remember, emotions are physical reactions to powerful thoughts. Are you telling yourself that if you're not perfect, you're a total failure? That if one person rejects you, no one will ever love you? Are you setting goals for yourself that are impossible, so that you're always letting yourself down? Once you've pinpointed what you're telling yourself, make a deliberate effort to try seeing your situation from a new perspective and telling yourself different messages.

► Seek God. There's nothing like telling God about what you're going through and reading the Bible to find fresh perspective. Jill says, "When I am depressed or worried about something that's gone wrong, reading the Bible always lifts my spirit." Spending time with God can help you see your problems in a new light.

▶ Nourish your sense of humor. Take a break and rent a funny video, watch a stupid sitcom, read a joke book. Doing this isn't the same as laughing away your pain. It's just putting things into perspective: "I feel bad, but bad feelings aren't going to dominate me. I still have my sense of humor. I can keep things in perspective."

▶ Wait it out. It sounds trite, but there's truth to the cliche, "This too shall pass." Though it seems impossible, you will put your life back together. You will survive. You will go on.

A Healthy Response to Grief

The suggestions above should help you deal with feelings caused by everyday losses and stresses. More significant losses—the death of a loved one, divorce, a major illness, even moving—usually require more time to work through. It's a process called mourning. And there are certain stages you go through.

▶ Denial. The initial reaction to a great loss is denial. If someone dies, you tell yourself it didn't really happen. If your parents divorce, you convince yourself they'll get back together. Your emotions go into shock, you feel numb. Denial can be useful for a time, while you rally your emotional forces to deal with the pain.

▶ Anger. After reality seeps in, and you realize your parents really aren't living together or your grandfather really is gone, you feel angry. It's a reaction to the helplessness and hurt you feel; you really can't control another person's life or death. During this stage you're preoccupied with the loss and what it means to you.

▶ Bargaining. Your prayers may take on a desperate, bargaining quality: "Dear God, if you just bring my parents back together, I'll never fight with them again." "If you'll fix it so we move back to the old town, I'll never cut classes again." But the bargaining doesn't work and the anger is intensified.

▶ Depression. Realizing that bargaining does no good and anger leads nowhere, you might become depressed for a time. You might not want to see people. You might feel guilty, imagining you had a part in whatever happened, or you may feel regret over things you didn't do. This can be a time of coming to grips with the fact of your loss, which can lead into the final stage.

▶ Acceptance. You come to grips with your loss and the true meaning of the loss for you. Slowly you're able to let go of the anger, guilt and depression. You begin to pick up the pieces of your life—forever altered by what happened, but able to go on.

These stages take time to work through, and you may find yourself moving back and forth among them. If you're facing a serious loss, give yourself the time and space to go through your grief, and seek help if you need it.

Depression: When Blue Turns to Black

Think of depression as catching an emotional cold. When you have the emotional sniffles, you feel gloomy, sad, dejected for a day or two or three. But eventually it passes. If it doesn't, it's time to seek help. Your "sniffles" may be developing into the emotional equivalent of pneumonia—a serious depression.

If you've tried the suggestions for beating the blues and they don't work, or you find yourself stuck in the mourning process, you may need help from a trained professional. If the following warning signs describe you, get yourself help. (If they sound like someone you know, strongly urge your friend to get help. Or confide your concern in an adult—the friend's parents, or some trusted adult.)

Depression's Danger Signals

▶ Isolating yourself. Do you find yourself turning down invitations to go out with friends, and wanting to be alone all the time?

► Changes in sleeping patterns. Do you have trouble getting to sleep at night? Do you wake up during the night with a feeling of dread, and have trouble getting back to sleep? Do you wake up early in the morning, still tired, but unable to go back to sleep? Do you feel tired even after spending extra hours in bed?

► Finding it difficult to concentrate. Do you read a page and find that you're unaware of what you've read? Do you find it difficult, or nearly impossible, to function in your classes?

► Loss of interest in activities. Do you find the things you used to enjoy no longer appeal to you? Do you feel you just don't want to try anymore?

► Thoughts of suicide. It's normal to fantasize about how much people will miss you when you're gone. But if suicide is often on your mind, and you plan out how you would do it, this is a serious danger sign.

► Pervasive, overwhelming feelings of shame, self-hatred, worthlessness, disappointment, guilt, blame, rage, helplessness or hopelessness.

► Self-destructive behavior such as drug and alcohol abuse, reckless driving, antisocial behavior such as vandalism, promiscuity, or stealing.

► Obsession with your health, or with food.

How to Find Help

It may not be easy to approach someone and say, "I need help." But don't think it's a sign of weakness to do so. It takes greater courage to find help than it does to shrink into yourself and do nothing.

Where should you start looking for help?

If you can, talk to your parents. Explain how you're feeling and why you think you may need professional help.

If you feel you can't talk to a parent or another close relative, find a youth leader or pastor, a teacher, school counselor or doctor and tell them how you feel and that you're looking for help. If they can't help you themselves, they can steer you to someone who can.

The yellow pages of your phone book list social service agencies, mental health facilities, family and children's agencies, psychiatrists, psychologists and social workers. Almost all of these professionals will see an adolescent at least once without requiring parental permission. If therapy is to continue and parental permission is required, no professional will share what you confide with anyone, including parents, unless you approve.

No matter how bad you feel, you can work through it and get better, with help. Don't deny yourself that help if you need it.

Jealousy: The Green-eyed Monster

Jeffrey knows about jealousy. He says, "In the past, my best friend and I sometimes went too far with our competitiveness. We'd try to outdo each other in everything from grades to clothes to who we hung around with."

Michelle can relate: "Though I am a musician myself, I'm still jealous of others who are more musically talented than I."

Basically, jealousy (or envy) rises when someone has something you want but can't have. Trendy clothes, for example, or a CD player, or a special friendship.

Have you ever forgotten that you're the fastest runner in your class because you were mad you lost the high jump to Marty? Or ever suddenly hated all your clothes—even that red sweater you received so many compliments on—because you couldn't keep up with Janet's stylish outfits? If so, you've discovered how jealousy distorts our view.

It's similar to how a near-sighted student's clear vision is shortened without his glasses. The whole world becomes blurry, except for the things that are within three feet of his face. He can't see the writing on the chalkboard. He can't even tell whether his girlfriend is smiling at him from across the classroom!

When you feel jealous, all that you have gets lost in the blur of your emotions. You begin to focus only on what you lack—and suddenly these things seem necessary for your happiness. You might even exaggerate, thinking that you're the only one who doesn't have everything you want.

Overcoming Envy

When you become jealous, admit it. Then try to get perspective:

▶ If you're a Christian, your identity is in Christ, not in what you own or have. Read the entire book of Ephesians and 2 Corinthians 4:8–18 for proof.

▶ You can't own anyone. If you're jealous over a friend, ask God to help you trust him to supply even your friendship needs. Also, pray that you'll let go of your fears of losing this person.

▶ Most things in life aren't "all or nothing" situations. Just because your best friend makes a new friend doesn't mean she suddenly has quit caring about you. And maybe you're not as smart as "Straight A" Stan, but you still have intelligence.

Now, take action:

▶ Ask yourself: Why do I feel jealous? Try to figure out what you feel you lack.

▶ Do a values check. Especially when you're envious of outward things such as money or good looks, ask: "Is this what matters most to me?" And read the book of Ecclesiastes and 1 Corinthians chapter 3 for God's view of what's really important.

▶ Count your blessings. Think about all the good things in your life: friends, family, intelligence, a healthy body, your abilities. . . .

▶ Consider talking to a friend about it.

▶ Get to know some of the people you're envious of. You'll find they have problems and fears, too.

▶ Write out your feelings. Then tear the letter up and throw it away, telling God you want him to help you do the same with your jealousy.

When You Feel Guilty

Let's say a friend falsely accuses you of gossiping. No reason to feel guilty for that. Or maybe you're shy and kids at school think you're a snob. Again, you have no reason to feel guilty. Or possibly you can't get above a C in English—no matter how hard you try. Again, declare yourself not guilty.

Consider these don'ts:

▶ Don't feel guilty if you know you're innocent of wrongdoing. No matter what anybody else thinks, you know the truth. And if it's true you're not guilty, you're not guilty.

▶ Don't feel guilty for not living up to another's expectations. Doing your best is good enough.

▶ Don't feel guilty for not living up to your own expectations. An A in math isn't all that important. Failing to make JV your freshman year doesn't mean you're a failure. Raising your hand and giving a wrong answer isn't a crime. Don't be so hard on yourself.

▶ Don't feel guilty over stupid stuff. So what if your team lost at Trivial Pursuit because you didn't know the National Anthem for Bulgaria. That's nothing to feel guilty over. After all, it's only a game.

► Don't feel guilty if God doesn't think you're guilty. God is the one who set the standards for right and wrong. If God doesn't find you guilty for a certain action, then you're not guilty. Ask yourself: Does God's book say what I'm doing is wrong? If not, then you're free to be guilt free.

When Guilt Won't Go Away

Consider an illustration: Imagine you're finally sixteen and you have your driver's license to prove it. For your birthday, your parents buy you a new convertible sports car. You grab the keys, start the engine, put down the top and head for the highway. The air smells fresh, the sun shines brightly. As you roll along, the engine purrs like a contented lion. Life couldn't be better.

Suddenly it starts to rain. You pull over. But before you raise the top, the interior gets pretty wet. Suddenly the drive isn't much fun anymore: no sunshine, no warm breeze, no fresh air. If that isn't bad enough, muddy water splashes all over that once-shiny exterior. Then you realize something: The engine is purring as powerfully and contentedly as ever. In spite of the crummy circumstances, you know the engine is still working like the fine-tuned, powerful machine it was built to be. The car is still a great car—the engine proves it. You smile, lean back, and before long, you're once again enjoying the ride—and feeling good.

Now the point. A sports car's finely crafted engine is like this basic fact: If you are a Christian, you are no longer guilty. Because of your friendship with Christ, God has forgiven you—totally. True, you may not feel forgiven at times. You may occasionally feel pretty lousy. Yet in spite of how you feel, the "engine runs smoothly." That is, the fact of our forgiveness remains true. God continues to accept and love us. In knowing this, you can lean back, relax, and before long, you'll once again "enjoy the ride"—and the good feelings.

When You Are Guilty

There are times when we should feel guilty—because we are guilty. We have done something that God says is clearly wrong. Does God suddenly point a righteous finger and say: "Guilty as charged!" Not exactly. He still loves us, we still have our friendship with Jesus, he still forgives us. Yet while the friendship is not broken, it is strained—and we have strained it. As a result, we don't feel at ease with our friendship anymore. In a word, we feel guilt—very real guilt. Until we make some changes, we will continue to feel guilt and our friendship will suffer. But God doesn't want it that way. He wants to make our friendship with Jesus strong and healthy again. Here's how:

▶ Say you're sorry (1 John 1:9). God's book calls it confession. It's telling God you're genuinely sorry. That is, "I'm sorry and I mean it!"

▶ Do a turn around (Ezekiel 18:30). This is what God's book calls repentance. Here's the idea. Imagine you're walking down the hall toward English class. Suddenly you realize you're headed in the wrong direction. You're supposed to be going to history class—and that's at the opposite end of the hall. So you do a 180-degree turn and head in the right direction. That's what repentance is. You're headed in the wrong direction, you realize your mistake, and you turn around and head in the right direction. In doing so, you move away from whatever caused the guilt.

▶ Seek forgiveness from others. You prove—or disprove—your friendship with God through your friendship with others (Matthew 5:23–24). If you say "I'm sorry" to God, are you willing to say "I'm sorry" to someone you've wronged?

▶ Believe it. What if you don't feel forgiven? God promises forgiveness to those who sincerely ask for it (1 John 1:9). It's a fact—regardless of how we feel. For a good reminder, refer back to "When Guilt Won't Go Away."

"Do you remember *me*, Ed? Freshman ... biology?"

"Nothing But Gray": Anxiety

Wouldn't it be great to wake up tomorrow morning and know exactly where you should go to college, or what classes to sign up for next year? Or to find under your pillow a list of the people who will be true friends to you throughout high school?

Such answers would certainly make life easier. But as you know, there are no guarantees. The next few years offer no sure bets apart from God. Yet you can learn to live in the uncertain world of high school. Here's how to turn your anxiety from a vague gray into a clearer, better-defined picture that will allow you to make good choices.

Stop and Ask

Ask yourself these six questions any time you're in a scary or painful situation:

▶ Can I realistically do anything to change this situation? If the answer is yes, then do what you can to change it. If the answer is no, then you have to learn to accept things as they are and put it all in God's hands.

▶ What can I control? You can never control people, situations, or results. But you will always be able to change your own attitude, your knowledge of the facts, and your actions. You'll worry a lot less if you will concentrate only on what you can control.

▶ What are my strengths in this situation? Understanding what you're capable of will give you confidence, and confidence dispels anxiety.

▶ What can I accomplish? Deciding on a specific goal does two things: It helps you know what direction to head in, and it makes decisions easier by giving you an idea of your priorities—what's ultimately most important. Just remember to set realistic "stretch" goals that challenge and motivate you, rather than unrealistic "strain" goals that cause you to get tense and panic.

▶ What do I have to do right now? Focus on the job at hand. Worrying about the things you need to do tomorrow will only get in the way of what you're trying to finish today.

Relaxers

Sometimes the worries will get to you. Tests, friendships, future decisions, getting along with Mom and Dad—they all come with their own kind of pressure. So try these stress-busters next time you're feeling anxious, and give yourself a chance to clear your mind.

▶ Take a nap.
▶ Call a friend and talk.
▶ Take a bath or shower.
▶ Go for a bike ride or a walk.
▶ Read a book that interests you.
▶ Play music you enjoy.
▶ Write your concerns out.

▶ Read the Bible and pray.
▶ Do something fun with a friend.
▶ Exercise.
▶ Write an old friend.
▶ Scream into a pillow or out in the car.
▶ Go to the mall and window shop or people-watch.

An Extra Help

That "I'm-worried-because-I'm-not-sure-what's-best" feeling is common to everyone. But for Christians, God has given us an additional way to defeat anxiety: the gift of himself—the only sure thing in heaven or on earth—and his promise that he will both supply our needs and love us, no matter what.

And that should be the greatest reassurance of all.

The Good Side of Bad Feelings

As hard as it might be to believe, feeling bad has its good side. Consider:

▶ Sometimes bad feelings lead you to take action. Bump against a car exhaust and you jump away—saving yourself from a severe burn. Cut your hand on a saw in shop class and you stop sawing—avoiding serious injury. Your nervous system serves you well, "shouting" at you when you're in danger.

Bad feelings are a lot like that. When you feel stressed out, it's a warning to slow down. When you feel angry, it's a sign that you need to take care of something that's bothering you. When you feel envious, it's a signal that you need to refocus your friendship on caring and respect, away from competition and rivalry. Bad feelings sound the alarm, calling you to take action.

▶ Sometimes bad feelings reveal your need to trust God. Imagine this: A tourist leaves his experienced guide to explore the picturesque mountainside. He steps confidently onto the edge and the rocks slip from under him, leaving him dangling helplessly over a thousand-foot drop. He screams in terror and miraculously the guide shows up, lifting him to safety.

Do you ever feel like the tourist? You go along, feeling you're handling school, family, friendships pretty well without God's guidance. Then all of a sudden something goes wrong—maybe a best friendship collapses or your family seems to be crumbling to pieces—and you are left dangling from the "edge" of your emotions. When that happens you feel the need to cry out for your "trusted guide"—for help from the God who always knows what's best for you. And in seeking his help and strength during rough times, you may discover something else: He is a valuable companion even when life doesn't seem so bad.

► Sometimes bad feelings reveal your need for others. When you reach high school, there is obviously a need for greater independence. But occasionally the rough times and bad feelings are a reminder that you still need the guidance, love, and even gentle hug of a friend, parent, or other trusted adult.

► Sometimes bad feelings help you grow. A short time ago, your body went through some pretty dramatic changes. When those "growing pains" ceased, however, you found yourself a bit taller and a lot more physically mature. Now think about bad feelings. Your emotional aches and pains can result in a good deal of personal growth. Consider these examples: Hard times can teach us to stick to what we feel is true and right (James 1:2–4). They can lead us to be more at ease when circumstances get crummy (Philippians 4:12–13). Hard times can even help us to see the positive side of our own weaknesses (2 Corinthians 12:7–10).

► Sometimes bad feelings cause us to be more sensitive to another's pain. Groups like Alcoholics Anonymous are effective because people who've "been there" offer support and encouragement for the struggling alcoholic. It's the same with our own hard times. If we've "been there," we're naturally more sensitive, caring, and encouraging toward those who are in the middle of some very tough times.

What about Feeling Good?

Gliding down the steep slope, Matt felt the cold, crisp air sting his face. He could hear nothing but the slicing sound the skis made on the sparkling, powdery snow. At times like these, Matt felt really alive. Truly happy. Then it happened. One week before a statewide skiing competition—a competition he'd trained for all winter—Matt twisted his knee. He was out for the season. In fact, the doctor said he might never compete again. Along with that, his hip-high cast itched continually and his crutches were nothing but a hassle. Needless to say, he was irritable and demanding, making life miserable for his parents and older sister.

As the weeks wore on, Matt still had his cast and crutches. Yet something was happening to his attitude. He started feeling a little less depressed; he could even joke about the accident. Matt admits the change had a lot to do with his family and friends. Even though he was not always pleasant to be around, his parents and sister spent more time than usual with him—making him feel somehow special. And as he lay on the couch, his mother brought him snacks and cleaned up after him. As a result, he came to appreciate his mom for all the little things she did for him.

Then there were his friends from church and school. The clutter of "get well" cards showed just how much they cared. Many of them even went out of their way to stop by and see him. While he still missed skiing, Matt started feeling pretty good. Even happy.

Of course, Matt could have stayed angry and bitter. He could have continued to feel cheated by his circumstances. He didn't do that. He decided not to dwell on the bad, but to look instead at the good that surrounded him. As a result, he learned to be more thankful for all he had. For Matt, the whole experience became a choice between happiness and anger. He chose happiness. He believes he made the right decision.

Seven Ways to Greater Happiness

Want to be truly happy? Then look here:

▶ Discover good friendships. The emphasis is on *good* friendships. Friendships based on mutual respect and solid friendship qualities are bound to make you happier.

▶ Treasure good memories. Spend some time thinking about last week. What were the little things that made you laugh, made you thankful, or made you feel accomplished? Doing this now and then can't help but make you feel good inside.

▶ Help others. Volunteer at a nursing home. Rake a neighbor's yard. Tutor a junior-high student. Do the dishes without being asked. You'll not only make someone happy, you'll go away feeling happy yourself.

▶ Seek alternatives. If what made you feel good is taken away, don't mope. Look for other things to make you happy.

▶ Do right. Stand up for your values and your faith. Doing so will make you feel very good about yourself.

▶ Discover contentment. We all like to be "bubbly happy." There's nothing wrong with that. But that's really not what true happiness is all about. True and lasting happiness is not fun like a roller coaster. It's more like an enjoyable, peaceful walk in the park. But it's even more than that. It's a willingness to accept circumstances as they are. While there may be problems and disappointments, true happiness helps you appreciate and be grateful for what you have.

▶ Go to the source. God is the source of true and lasting happiness. Talk to him, let him talk to you through his book, spend time with other Christians, enjoy his creation—all these things bring you closer to him. And closer to true happiness and real joy.

Feeling Good about Feeling in Love

When Mindy saw the guy at the movies, her heart pounded faster, her palms became sweaty, and she couldn't stop thinking about him all night long. Mindy knew she was in love.

Through a friend, Mindy learned that the guy's name was Rob. The same friend also got the two together. For a while it was euphoria. Mindy and Rob couldn't see each other enough. Yet after a few weeks, Mindy wasn't so sure any more. True, some of the "love feelings" remained, yet something didn't seem right. There was Rob's jealousy—triggered even if she looked at another guy. He also acted pretty immature and had a bad temper. Before long, Mindy decided to call it quits. After all, there was this other guy in history class who made her heart pound faster, caused her palms to go sweaty. . . . This time she knew she was really in love.

Mindy, it could be said, was in love with being in love. That is, she liked the good feelings an attractive guy gave her. Like Mindy, we all get those "love feelings" when we're attracted to certain members of the opposite sex. Maybe it's blond hair. Maybe it's green eyes. Maybe it's a special kind of walk or talk.

Maybe it's those cool clothes. Whatever it is, it's pretty normal. Yet confusing love feelings with real love is like confusing Twinkies with health food. Junk food tastes good. Eat a whole box of Ding Dongs, however, and you're sick. Mistake your love feelings for real love and you're headed for trouble.

When you feel "in love" remember:

▶ Love feelings come and go. Enjoy love feelings while they last, but don't mistake them for the real thing. If you do, you're liable to make promises and say things you'll soon regret. Point: Love feelings should never say, "I love you and you alone—let's only date each other."

SHORTLY AFTER THEIR DATE BEGAN, LOU SENSED THAT HE WAS GETTING BAD VIBES FROM HELEN.

► Love feelings can't think straight. Ever know a guy whose girlfriend could always talk him into doing silly, stupid, and sometimes harmful stuff? When love feelings get charged up, the brain blows a fuse.

► Love feelings are conscience free. Love feelings can cause you to do things that are totally against your values. Don't let them dictate how far you go sexually. If they do, they—and you—won't stop.

► Love feelings focus on the outside. Real love, instead, centers on deeper, inner qualities.

► Love feelings are selfish. Love feelings are out for themselves. They want to make you feel good. In contrast, true love wants what's best for the other person.

► Love feelings are interested in mutual attraction. "I like how you look. You like how I look." That's the basis for love feelings. True love, on the other hand, seeks to discover mutual interests and shared values.

► Love feelings can be the start of a good relationship, but . . . Love feelings are obviously the way most if not all of us begin a relationship. But those feelings leave when your girlfriend has bad breath, when your boyfriend embarrasses you, when your romantic interest is late, when your girlfriend gains five pounds, etc. On the other hand, true love says: "I love you and respect you in spite of your shortcomings."

FRESHMAN LYMAN FELDNER'S CHANCES OF MAKING IT TO BIOLOGY LAB ON TIME WEREN'T LOOKING TOO HOT.

SECTION 3.

Caring for the You that Shows

LUKE GOLOBITSH

How Do You Like Your Body?

▶ Rick planned to go out for track in high school. He loved the running, but especially the hurdles. He relished pitting himself against others, against his own best speed, pushing himself and occasionally winning. Whenever Rick was upset about something, a good run always made him feel better.

▶ Jennifer loved to dance. While ballet and modern jazz were her favorites, any kind of dancing made her feel wonderful. Something about the way the music and the movement melded together. It transported her almost into another world.

▶ Jason was overweight, and felt terrible about it. Especially when he compared himself to Jim Patterson, who was molded to perfection. Every girl noticed Jim Patterson. People noticed Jason, too, but only to snicker at his bulges and his braces. Weight-lifting bored Jason, he was too clumsy to play football or basketball, and too chicken to wrestle. He began to hate not only his body, but his whole self.

How do you feel about your body? Is it a source of

WELCOME TO HIGH SCHOOL

joy or embarrassment to you? If you're like most people, it's a little of both.

You may relish some form of sports or other physical activity, but feel self-conscious about your acne or your weight.

You know your body is changing. The body, mind, and feelings are all connected, and so the physical changes cause lots of changes in how you feel about yourself and others, even the way you act. (Jason's self-consciousness affected his social life; he tended to shy away from making new friends, automatically assuming he'd be rejected because of his weight.)

Most of the physical and emotional changes are connected to hormones. Remember what we said about all the "voices" that tend to influence you? Well, in high school the voice of your body—mostly to the tune of your hormones—tends to come on with the power of heavy metal music. Nothing wrong with heavy metal music, necessarily—but if it blares too loudly, it can actually make you deaf. If you don't make sure you're the one controlling the volume and the equalizer, the heavy metal can make you deaf to every other voice—including God's and your own good judgment.

You'll need that sense of control, because you'll face opportunities and temptations like never before. For example, with sex.

You think about sex a lot; you can't help it. Your friends are talking about sex, and it seems like they actually have experience. (Sometimes they do, sometimes they just pretend to.) You hear in your sex education and health classes about sexually transmitted diseases and AIDS. You hear people say you shouldn't have sex "until you're ready." How do you know if you're "ready"? If you decide to wait until marriage, will you be labeled a homosexual, or rejected as undatable?

There will be opportunities and temptations to experiment—with alcohol, with drugs. With sex. With reckless driving. With diets. With steroids.

When you were a kid, you could blame things on your parents: "My mother says I can't do that." In high school, you can't say, "No, I won't do drugs because my mother won't let me." You're expected to take more responsibility for your choices, big and little. Mom probably no longer nags you to brush your teeth or eat your greens. It may seem wonderful to be able to choose potato chips over broccoli every time—until the pounds start adding up and you realize that your choices really do matter.

They matter to you, because you will feel the consequences almost immediately. But what you do with your body may well affect others. If you drink and drive, you may end up killing someone. If you're promiscuous, you risk giving yourself and someone else a sexually transmitted disease. It's not always easy to think ahead about the possible consequences of decisions you make, but doing so is one way to strengthen your own resolve to do some things and not do other things.

Your decisions matter a great deal to one other person—God. He is interested and aware of every little detail. As a great poet put it (in the Bible): "You know when I sit and when I rise" (Psalm 139:2). God made human beings, body included, and called it all good. The Bible says he actually comes to dwell inside our bodies, and that what we do to our bodies we in effect do to Jesus Christ himself. (See 1 Corinthians 6:15.) God thinks the body is good; he made us with the ability to revel in the gamut of sights, sounds, tastes, smells, and the many sensations of touch that are possible. He gave us guidelines to help us use our bodies wisely, so that they become a source of pleasure and not pain. "Do not offer the parts of your body to sin, as instruments of wickedness, but rather offer yourselves to God, as those who have been brought from death to life; and offer the parts of your body to him as instruments of righteousness. Don't you know that you yourselves are God's temple and that God's Spirit lives in you? Therefore honor God with your body" (Romans 6:13; 1 Corinthians 3:16, 6:20).

This idea that God dwells within you, if you're a Christian, can profoundly affect the decisions you make. Not only in the obvious ways, such as how you respond to temptations to abuse alcohol or drugs or sex. But also in the way you think about your looks.

When You're Not One of the "Beautiful People"

Magazines, television, movies, and books all remind us of what we should be after: the ideal body. Flawless skin, straight teeth, shiny hair. Curves or muscles in all the right places, and above all, no flab. And there's plenty of advice, mostly from advertisers, on how to make it happen: Just use this moisturizer or this cleanser, and you'll have flawless skin. Work out with these Universal machines and your muscles will bulge. Just try this diet plan and you'll lose ten pounds in a week.

The goal of all our efforts: Once we have the ideal body, we'll never be lonely again. Beautiful people from the opposite sex will compete with each other for our attention.

We pursue madly, a dream. A lie. The truth is, only a very small number of people are capable of getting the so-called "ideal look." The kind of body in our jeans depends first of all on the genes in our body— and we can't change those.

For most of us, the "perfect body" is an impossible goal. Try to reach it and you'll be pulled into a never-ending cycle of discouragement and misery.

There is a better way. You have a choice. It all depends on whose standards of looking good you accept—Hollywood's or God's. The view you choose will determine how you define looking good.

A Healthy Definition of Beauty

God doesn't seem to share our standard of beauty. We value leanness, oval faces, regular features. God seems to take delight in one thing: variety. The proof? He wired each of us to be a particular shape, height, even weight. And while we can't do anything about our inborn structure, we can control how we think about what we're born with. This, in turn, will influence how we feel about our body.

We can swallow the lie, try to reshape our bodies to look like a model, fail, then hate ourselves for not being perfect. Or we can reject "the ideal," realize that God made us with the exact body we have and loves us just as we are.

Taking Care of What You Have

As a freshman in high school, Kathy hardly stood out as one of the "beautiful people." At first glance, she seemed rather plain. She didn't wear overly fashionable clothes and didn't own a pair of designer gym shoes. She used little makeup. While not overweight, Kathy's hips and waist were larger than many of the other girls in her class. Yet one thing about Kathy stood out: her impeccable neatness. Her hair always shone and smelled fresh, and her clothes always fit extremely well. And while she never tried to be a beauty queen, she did care about doing the best with what she had. She obviously took pride in the body God had given her. It showed.

There was something else about Kathy. When you were with her, you just knew she accepted you—body imperfections and all. As a result, Kathy was the kind of person you liked to be around.

Eating Disorders: The Problem of Body Hate

Most of us dislike something about our bodies. Some of us, however, literally hate the way we look. That can lead to trouble—very big trouble. Like anorexia and bulimia. In order to "slim down," girls (and a small number of guys) with anorexic eating disorders will go on starvation diets and abuse diet pills and laxatives. As for bulimics, they'll eat obsessively, then stick their fingers down their throats to "purge" themselves of food. Girls with eating disorders literally try starving themselves into thinner, more "perfect" bodies. But no matter how skinny and emaciated they get, they never become thin enough. With ribs showing and breasts shrunken, a girl suffering from an eating disorder will look in a mirror and still hate herself for being fat and ugly.

When this is the case, the problem of self-hatred has gone very, very deep. If this describes you or someone you know, professional help is needed immediately. Talk to a trusted adult who can help find the counseling you or a suffering friend may need. Do it now—before it's too late.

Steroids: When We Love Our Bodies Too Much

When he started high school, Michael was spending hours in his basement working out with weights. In time, he became obsessed with his quickly developing muscles—so obsessed that he couldn't walk by a mirror without flexing. And his muscular frame was pretty impressive. By the time he graduated, he'd competed and placed in local body building contests.

When Michael started college, the competition suddenly became stiffer. Other body builders were edging by him—their muscles larger, more clearly defined. Their secret: steroids. Wanting what they had, Michael started using steroids. It didn't take long for the drug to "bulk him up." It also didn't take long for the steroids to have other effects. He began suffering severe mood swings, going from anger to depression. Then there was the acne that started covering his back. His urine turned dark brown and he often felt sharp pains in his groin. There were also leg cramps, so painful that he would wake up screaming in the night. At one point, his heart pounded so hard during a workout that he knew he was going to die. Finally, after four years of steroid abuse, Michael gave up the drug. He realized the destruction he was causing his body. He also realized that there were far more important things in life than seeking that perfect look. Like family, friendship, and his relationship with God. "My obsession with my body," Michael now says, "was a waste of time."

Facts about the "Perfect Body Drug"

Some things you should know about anabolic steroids:

▶ Stunts natural body growth. It's ironic: Steroids are touted as a growth hormone for building bigger bodies, yet these drugs prematurely stop natural body growth. Using steroids may in fact leave you shorter than you were meant to be.

▶ Mood swings. Violent, uncontrollable behavior and chronic depression can result from steroid use.

▶ Increased acne. Many users experience severe acne during use.

▶ Harmful to sexual development. Steroids decrease the natural level of the male hormone testosterone, which sometimes produces a lower sperm count and can reduce the natural sex drive.

▶ Balding. Steroid use can lead to permanent balding before the age of twenty-five.

▶ Heart and liver disorders. Steroid use increases the chance of heart attacks, liver cancer, and other serious physical disorders.

▶ Milk-producing breasts in guys. The results of using this so-called macho drug can certainly be far from macho.

The Wonder that You Are

Maybe you don't like your nose, or the color of your hair, or the size of your feet, but all in all your body is really an amazing creation. Want proof of the wonder that you are?

▶ Your brain's neuron circuitry is 1,400 times more complex than the entire world's telephone system.

▶ No one in the world has a voice just like yours.

▶ Your fingertips are so sensitive that they can feel a pressure of less than 1/1,400 of an ounce (the average weight of a fly).

▶ Your face is capable of more than 250,000 movements.

▶ At rest, your heart beats an average of 104,000 times a day, pumping approximately 2,100 gallons of blood through your system in a 24-hour period. It puts out enough energy in that time to lift nearly 2,000 pounds 41 feet off the ground.

▶ By age 70, your brain will have filed away at least 100 trillion pieces of information. The entire Encyclopedia Britannica contains only 200 million bits of information.

▶ Most people can detect and recognize some 4,000 distinctly different scents.

Your Body Matters to God

Even if you don't like all of you, there's good reason to take care of yourself: God wants you to.

He made the body, figure, and face that you have and called all of it "good." And he has set up residence inside you if you're a Christian. Christ gave up his life out of love for you, because he valued you. He takes healthy pride in your fitness and looks. So should you.

Feeling Great and Looking Good

Looking and feeling your best is a matter of care and cleanliness: When you eat right, exercise, and practice good hygiene, you feel better. Healthier. And you'll almost certainly like yourself more in the long run.

That's what happened to Shannon. More than a year ago, she lost twenty-five pounds over several months. Shannon didn't change her eating habits drastically, and she didn't skip meals, but she ate only low-fat foods and avoided sweets. She also jogged every other day. "Before I lost weight," she says, "I was tired all the time, I didn't like the way I looked, and I didn't appreciate my body at all. But as the pounds came off and exercise became a regular part of my life, I discovered new energy that would last the entire day. I no longer craved desserts and candy bars. And I began to like myself and my body better."

CARING FOR THE YOU THAT SHOWS

Pounds to Go

To lose weight you must avoid the junk food snack scene. Especially at first, though, you may find that difficult. Try these ideas if you're having trouble:

▶ Brush your teeth. Few things go well with that toothpaste taste.

▶ Exercise. Surprisingly, exercise decreases your appetite, and usually your craving for sweets.

▶ Work on a project. It will get your mind off of food.

▶ Feed your mind. Read a good book or magazine.

▶ Clean your closet. Trying to squeeze into all the clothes you've "outgrown" may help you think twice before you head for the refrigerator.

▶ Snack, but on something nutritious. Grapes, for example, or graham crackers, or low-fat frozen yogurt.

Also: A lot of people count calories to lose weight. Instead, pay more attention to the content of the food you eat rather than the quantity. Foods high in fat (mayonnaise, butter, anything fried, most cheeses and desserts) add more pounds than equal amounts of low-fat foods (fruits and vegetables, skinless chicken or turkey, whole wheat bread, most fish, pasta, frozen yogurt, and rice).

Don't forget to eat a balanced diet, either—something you've heard since you started school. The U.S. Department of Agriculture suggests the following for teenagers each day:

- ▶ 3 to 4 servings of milk/dairy products
- ▶ 2 servings of meat/protein
- ▶ 4 servings of fruits/vegetables
- ▶ 4 servings of bread/cereal

Getting Fit

Exercise is the second part of the picture. You probably know someone who spends three hours a day working out at the local health club. Fortunately, getting in shape doesn't have to take that much time. You'll actually notice results if you exercise for thirty minutes or so (including time for warming up and stretching) three or four times a week.

There are two types of exercise: aerobic and non-aerobic. Aerobic activities such as walking, running, jogging, swimming, skating, bicycling, jump rope, singles' tennis, soccer, basketball, and cross-country skiing improve your endurance, strengthen your heart and lungs, and help you lose weight. You benefit if you do them long enough to raise your heartbeat to the 140 to 175 beats per minute range, and keep it there for twenty minutes.

Non-aerobic exercise is good for building speed or agility but not so much for losing weight. Such activities include baseball, football, gymnastics, dancing, and weight lifting.

For example, a 105- to 115-pound teenager burns 1.7 calories per minute (cpm) while studying. But if you'll go for a brisk walk, you can use up 5.4 cpm. Here are some other activities and their cpm rates.

- ▶ slow walking 3.9
- ▶ swimming (casual) 4.0
- ▶ water skiing 5.0
- ▶ biking 5.4
- ▶ doubles' tennis 5.6
- ▶ aerobic dancing 5.8
- ▶ stair climbing 5.9
- ▶ basketball (half-court) 7.3
- ▶ volleyball 7.8
- ▶ jogging 8.6
- ▶ cross-country skiing 9.2
- ▶ jumping rope 13.3

For Non-athletes Who Want to Exercise

"Athletic" may be the last word anyone would use to describe you. Yet there's sure to be an activity that will fit your personality and preferences, and help you stay fit at the same time. You just need to find what works for you. Consider these:

▶ Add music to your workouts.

▶ If you don't want the pressure of competing and you like to work at your own pace, maybe you should exercise by yourself.

▶ If you're one who needs a structured plan to help you be disciplined, join an aerobics class or use home videos.

▶ Start with a simple activity that doesn't demand a lot of skill, like jumping rope or walking.

► Do you prefer to practice something until you master it? Try skating, skiing, racquet sports, or almost any sport that uses a ball.

► If competition motivates you, join a team or work out with a friend.

► Some people like scenery and open spaces when they exercise. If you're that way, do your thing outdoors.

If Acne's a Problem

Good health habits will greatly help another very common teenage problem: acne. Stress, poor diet, and lack of hygiene can all aggravate acne. But none of these conditions cause it. Acne is a skin disorder, not a "normal teenage condition." It's common in the teenage years because hormones stimulate the oil glands deep in the skin's pores. In some people something else happens at the same time to cause the acne: the skin cells deep inside the pore clump together. Then the blackhead or whitehead is formed. If that gets inflamed, you see the red zit.

If you have acne, follow these do's and don'ts:

▶ Be extremely careful of what you put on your face. Cosmetics, sunscreens, moisturizers and even hair products usually contain ingredients that aggravate acne tremendously. Sadly, even some acne medications contain ingredients that actually make acne worse! Be scrupulous about reading labels. Here is a list of ingredients to avoid, no matter what the product:

—lanolin in any form.

—isopropyl myristate. This is a penetrating oil that is actually used in Liquid Wrench! Other forms of this type of skin pollutant: isopropyl palmitate, butyl stearate, isopropyl isostearate, isostearyl neopenta-noate, myristyl myristate, decyl oleate, octyl stearate, octyl palmitate, isocetyl stearate, PPG 2 myristyl propionate.

—laureth-4 and sodium lauryl sulfate, found in some acne medications.

—D & C pigments, commonly used in blushers.

—mineral oil and other oils.

► Use mild soap to wash your face, two or three times a day. No need to use special acne soaps. Acne is a problem deep within the pores, not on the surface.

► Use acne medications correctly. Benzoyl peroxide is the best. (However, make sure you read your labels, and avoid anything that has the above ingredients or that promises to moisturize at the same time. Benoxyl, Topex, Dry and Clear seem to be safe.) Start with a five percent concentration. Apply it thirty minutes after you wash your face, and apply it all over the area where you tend to break out, whether there are pimples there or not. Benzoyl peroxide works to prevent zits by helping your skin to peel deep down, and by killing bacteria deep within the pore. Therefore, your goal is to get to the point where your skin is gently peeling and flaking. This goes against all the advice in the beauty magazines, but it's the only way to clear acne. If you want to clear up acne, you need to dry out your skin a little. At first, you may only be able to keep the medication on for a couple of hours. Slowly build up the time you wear it until you get to the point where your skin is gently peeling. By this time, you should be clearing up. (Be patient; it usually takes six to twelve weeks.) Drying your skin won't cause wrinkling; it will prevent acne scarring.

▶ Don't use moisturizers. If your skin gets too red and irritated from the benzoyl peroxide, stop using it for a day or two. Moisturizers worsen acne.

▶ Keep yourself healthy. A good diet, low in fat and refined sugar and high in whole grains, fruits, and vegetables will go a long way not only in helping your acne, but in keeping your weight down and helping you feel better. Some people are also helped by taking 100 mg. of zinc a day. And, since stress aggravates acne, exercise and taking time to relax is a good idea.

▶ Keep your hands away from your face. Don't pick at your zits or rest your hands on your face.

▶ If all else fails, get some help. A very helpful book is *Dr. Fulton's Step-by-Step Program for Treating Acne* by Dr. James Fulton and Elizabeth Black (check your public library). This book has more details on how to clear your skin and how to find a competent dermatologist. You might also try a dermatologist who seems to be helping someone you know.

▶ Remember, you are more than your complexion. Don't let acne wreck your social life. Wear a smile, be friendly and outgoing, and others won't notice your problem nearly as much as you do.

The Problem of Drug Abuse

After talking to and surveying hundreds of high-school students, *Campus Life* magazine discovered that about ten out of every one hundred students regularly use illegal drugs. Think about this: If one person out of ten is using regularly, then three students in a class of thirty may have some kind of drug problems. And their problems affect everybody. Fighting, disruptive behavior, on-campus drug dealing are all symptoms of drug abuse—symptoms that hurt the spirit and reputation of the entire school.

Campus Life discovered something else: Drug use is not limited to the so-called "burnouts." Other students—from cheerleader to class president—are potential drug abusers, vulnerable to all the pain and addiction drugs can cause. Breaking down the "druggie" stereotype helps us realize two important things:

▶ We are all vulnerable to drug use—no matter what our background. When we realize our own vulnerability, we become more willing to protect ourselves. One of the best ways to do this is through drug education.

But education isn't enough. As you enter high school, you need to have your own good reasons for not using. Spend some time thinking about how your values and beliefs apply to your commitment not to use. Think about how the friends you have either help or hinder those values. By educating yourself and by thinking through your own values, you'll be better able to say no—and mean it.

▶ So-called druggies are people too. By looking at the real person behind the stereotype, we begin to see the real reasons he or she uses illegal drugs. When that's done, judgment stops and caring and understanding begin.

Why Students Use Drugs

The main reason most students give for using drugs (including alcohol) is experimentation or curiosity. Yet this reason is complicated by other reasons that aren't so obvious or easy to recognize. Such as:

▶ The influence of family. Students whose parents use drugs or alcohol have a much greater chance of addiction and substance abuse than those whose parents don't. If you live with drug or alcohol abusers, make a conscious decision right now not to follow in their steps.

▶ Friendship pressure. Drug users admit that friends greatly influence their choice to use drugs and alcohol. If your friends pressure you to drink or abuse drugs, it's time to look for new friends.

▶ Low self-worth. Students who feel unloved and unlovable often seek love and acceptance through partying with the partiers. Ironically, drug and alcohol abuse only add to those feelings of self-hate. Further, users almost always alienate themselves from friends who could actually bolster their self-worth. Do you have a low self-esteem? Then seek healthy relationships that affirm your worth and value. Most important, realize that God loves you right now just as you are.

▶ Escape. Substance abuse is no escape from life's hassles—it's only the path to more severe problems.

▶ Addiction. If you feel you need a drink on Friday night or if you know you just have to smoke marijuana with your friends after school, you are headed for very serious trouble. Seek help from a trusted adult right away.

When Alcohol Becomes the Drug of Choice

High-school students who claim they don't use "illegal drugs" often confess that they do drink. *Campus Life* surveys show that 56 percent of all high-school students drink alcohol at least occasionally. And a study done by the *American Journal of Public Health* claims that by age eighteen, nine out of ten guys and eight out of ten girls will drink at least once a month. Here's a fact: If you didn't drink throughout junior high or middle school, there's a good chance you'll begin drinking sometime in high school. Why? Consider:

▶ Increased opportunities. When you're in high school, you're on your own more than ever. Your parents no longer carry as much influence as they used to. On the other hand, your friends carry a great deal of influence. And if they drink, they're likely to influence you to do the same.

▶ You're more aware than ever that drinking is "acceptable." It's no secret that drinking is considered normal by most people. And even though adults say don't do it, their actions often say go ahead. Here's a challenge: When it comes to alcohol, make your own decisions apart from what even adults think or do.

▶ No reasons not to. Fear of punishment and fear of disappointing your parents don't mean as much as they did a year ago. You're ready to make some of your own decisions. If you don't have personal convictions against drinking, you'll have no real reason to say no.

What the Ads Don't Tell You About Alcohol and Cigarettes

Advertisements are out to con us. They feature beautiful young actors drinking wine coolers and having a great time. They show youthful models walking along the beach, delicately holding cigarettes. They spotlight rock stars singing praises of their favorite beer. Here's what they don't show or tell:

▶ Yellow teeth, stained fingers, bad breath, and smelly clothes. Not-so-beautiful signs of smoking.

▶ Accidents. Alcohol-related automobile accidents are the leading cause of death among teenagers.

▶ Acne. Drinking can increase acne and aggravate other skin-related problems.

▶ Lethal poisons. Among other things, cigarettes contain cyanide (a poison used to execute criminals) and nicotine (a highly addictive and poisonous substance). And in the smoke you'll find carbon monoxide, the same stuff that comes out of your car's exhaust.

▶ Flab. You'll never see a fat person in a beer ad— but you'll see plenty coming out of your local bar. Why? Alcoholic beverages are loaded with calories.

▶ Date rape and date abuse. You've heard the phrase: Don't drink and drive? Here's one just as important: Don't drink and date. Avoid date abuse, avoid compromising your values, avoid committing the terrible crime of rape (or being its victim). Keep alcohol out of romance.

▶ Addiction. The ability to "hold your liquor" should never be seen as a good sign. In fact, it's an indication that you may be headed for the serious problem of alcoholism—by far the worst problem of drug addiction in America today.

Looking for Real Fun?

A growing number of students across the country are out to prove there are plenty of fun and exciting things to do apart from drinking and drug abuse. Here are a few alternatives:

▶ Alcohol- and drug-free parties. Throw a party where fun—and not getting buzzed—is the chief goal. Be creative. Center around a theme, dress in goofy costumes, feature exotic or unusual food, show videos or make your own video movies.

▶ Be a positive thrill seeker. Explorer scouts and other recreation- and camping-oriented groups offer plenty of safe thrills and a lot of fun.

▶ Plan trips and activities through your youth group. Skiing, rappeling, trips to the local amusement parks—such thrilling and exciting activities are a great way to show your friends that fun doesn't have to be dangerous, unsafe, or illegal. Talk to your leader about building more fun into your youth group.

▶ Join a national movement. "Students Staying Straight" is a national movement of students who aren't afraid to say no to drug and alcohol use. If you'd like information on how to get your entire school involved, write: Project 714, P.O. Box 8936, Chattanooga, TN 37411.

When You're Asked to Drink or Use Drugs

Here are a few tips adapted from the Students Staying Straight handbook:

▶ Give a reason. Let people know why you don't do drugs or drink. Keep it simple: "No thanks, I don't drink—I don't believe it's good for me." But whatever you say, don't put others down.

▶ Have something else to do. If you're asked to drink or do drugs, suggest an alternative.

▶ Avoid tempting situations. Avoid parties where you know or suspect there'll be alcohol or drugs.

▶ Change the subject. Sometimes another person will realize you're not interested if you switch the subject: "No thanks, I don't want to. Listen, let's go check out the game."

▶ Accept the possibility of rejection. Rejection may come, but remember: Real friends want what's best for each other—and that doesn't include drug and alcohol abuse.

Love, Sex, and High School

With the increased freedom you have in high school, no doubt sooner or later you'll come up against the question of what to do about sex. There will be pressures: from your own desires, from friends, even from a society that (through the media) portrays sex as the most natural thing for two people who love each other. Let's look at these pressures and what to do about them.

The Pressure from Within

The pressure you feel from your own desires is a result of how God made you. He wired you to want to merge with the opposite sex, to want to touch, to be close, to love and be loved, to not be alone, to be naked and unashamed.

The Bible is very frank about sex. A whole book (the Song of Solomon) celebrates the sensuality of erotic love. But if God gave us the desire, he also gave us guidelines for making sure it leads to happiness and not pain.

The Bible's view of sex can be put quite simply: Sex is wonderful within marriage. Outside marriage, it's an offense to the One who invented it. Hebrews 13:4 says, "Marriage should be honored by all, and the marriage bed kept pure."

"Pure" means "unmixed with any other substance." To paraphrase, then: "Set your hopes and dreams on marriage. And into that marriage bed allow only one person—your husband or your wife. Don't adulterate that relationship with anyone else—not even the ghosts of past relationships."

God not only gives us the guidelines, he gives us the ability to follow them, if we ask him. In practical terms, here are some things you can do:

▶ Draw the line at your wedding day, and nowhere else. Having a clear-cut, no-nonsense standard means you don't have to check your feelings to see whether you'll say no this time. The wedding day is a good test. When the two of you are ready to get up in church and say, "I do," there is a pretty good chance you are serious enough to take the serious step of sex. If you're not ready for the wedding, you're not ready for sex.

▶ Draw up a detailed timetable for your goals. Take some time to start planning for your education, your career, your involvement with church and community, your hopes for marriage and family. While you may well change your plan later, having one will help you develop a sense of self-worth. It will help you think toward the future, and you'll be much less likely to risk the future for a few minutes of pleasure here and now.

▶ Pray that God will mold your values. God is the master craftsman who made you, who wants you to enjoy sex fully when the time is right. He can make a difference in your internal attitude. Begin to pray that he'll do this. Make your prayers specific—perhaps by relating them to the life-plan you've drawn up. For example, some people begin praying daily for their (unknown) future spouse, asking God to prepare them both for each other.

Saying No to the Crowd

You will probably encounter, sooner or later, pressures from friends to engage in sex. Sometimes it comes when your two best friends become sexually active. Whether they tell you the details or not, you know their lives are different. And they seem to have no regrets. You feel left behind, the odd one out.

Being in the minority isn't easy. Especially when you feel the full force of TV, movies, and music going against you, all seeming to assume that sex before marriage is as natural as getting a driver's license.

But you may not be in such a minority as you think. Those who consider sex a normal, healthy part of adolescence tend to speak up about it. Those who don't agree tend to consider the subject private. If you did some research, you'd probably find plenty of people who believe in waiting for marriage.

To go against the crowd, any crowd, you must have self-confidence. There are ways to build your self-confidence:

▶ Write out your philosophy of sex. It may help to first read some Christian books on the subject. (Recommended: *Worth the Wait; Love, Sex, and the Whole Person;* and *A Love Story*—all by Tim Stafford. *Next Time I Fall in Love,* by Chap Clark. *Handling Your*

Hormones, by Jim Burns.) But try to put your philosophy into your own words. Know what you believe, and why.

▶ Find some friends who share your philosophy. You may find them in high-school-oriented Christian clubs like Student Venture or Campus Life, or in a church youth group. Or you may simply find them one by one. Share your philosophy of sex with them, and ask them to tell you what they believe. If possible, agree to support each other in prayer.

▶ Put sex on your list of prayer concerns. Make it a daily prayer—whether you're under pressure or not—to be helped and guided on your way to a fulfilling sex life within marriage. Too often, prayers deal only with immediate requests. Pray long term. Prayer is a powerful tool for strengthening your basic values.

Setting Limits

Once you get into a relationship, it helps to ease potential pressure if you set some limits and talk through them. Here are some guidelines:

1. Anything you do physically—from holding hands on—is meant to express love. If an action doesn't express love, you don't want to do it no matter how good it feels.

2. You don't want to do anything you'll later regret. If and when you go on to other partners, you don't want to carry a residue of guilt. You don't want to end up feeling that you're "used goods."

3. You want to keep control. Our bodies tend to push us onward, toward sex. It's a powerful force that

makes people go from kissing to caressing, from caressing to touching private parts, from touching to sex. In a sense you're always in control; nothing can make you do anything. But people do reach a point where they no longer want to keep control. They end up doing what they didn't want to.

If only the second and third point mattered, you'd be better off not doing anything until the wedding day—not even holding hands. But the first point—the expression of love—is important. We go out with the opposite sex to explore the feelings and experiences of love. Perhaps we don't need to express our love physically, but it's nice if we can. Love between male and female has a physical dimension, which we must learn to express wisely and well.

This raises a question: How far do you go to express your love? If you love each other a lot, do you have to go a lot further sexually to express that? Does touching private parts, for example, express love more than kissing?

Touching private parts may be more sexually intense, but that doesn't make it more loving. The more intense experiences have some negative effects built in. The further you go, the harder it is to stop. The further you go, the more likely it is you'll end up feeling guilty and used. Even if you don't lose control, you end up feeling frustrated. What's so loving about working your way into a sweat and then making yourselves hold back, leaving both of you frustrated?

So here's a recommendation: Draw the line at kissing. And don't kiss for too long at a time, either. Set a reasonable time limit. How long a kiss do you need to express your caring?

Also, keep your hands away from areas that clothes usually cover. Don't lie down. And make the most out of kissing and holding hands. It's really not depriving you of anything. In fact, if you can set your limits and forget about stretching them, it will make your relationship a lot more relaxed, a lot more fun and a lot more loving.

Saying No to a Special Person

You'd be better off if you never got involved with someone who doesn't share your values. But to be perfectly realistic, you probably will. Sometimes you will like him or her so much you'll go against your better judgment. Sometimes you'll both get carried away by your feelings. Sometimes, too, you just won't know his or her true values until you're involved. People don't usually write their sexual philosophy on their T-shirt.

So what do you say when someone puts on the pressure? Sometimes you need to break down your philosophy into bite-sized chunks:

The line: If you really love me, you'll show it by giving me all your love.

The answer: If you really love me, you'll show it by never again asking me to go against what I believe.

The line: It hurts to love you so much and yet hold back from expressing it. I feel so frustrated.

The answer: Love is worth some sacrifices.

The line: It will make our love grow.

The answer: I'm concerned with what it grows into.

The line: It will bring us closer.

The answer: Like it does people in Hollywood?

The line: Every other girl (guy) does it.

The answer: Then go out with her (him).

The line: If you're going to be so rigid, you may lose me.

The answer: Is that a threat? Losing someone who threatens me would be more gain than loss.

The best answer for someone putting on pressure: Good-bye!

A Word about Masturbation

Masturbation is common among teenagers, and it causes many a lot of guilt. How should you feel about this practice?

Sex as God intended it is meant to be shared as an expression of love between two people in marriage. Since masturbation is solo sex, it falls short of this ideal. The common feelings of guilt and the tendency to masturbate to pornographic fantasies suggest that something isn't what it ought to be.

But very few people want to masturbate. They do it because they feel they can't help it.

The Bible doesn't say a thing about masturbation. This is significant, because the Bible isn't shy about sex. It forbids sex between family members, sex with a person of your own gender, sex with animals, sex with a person you're not married to. But not a word about masturbation. At the very least, the silence proves that masturbation is not on top of God's agenda.

If you struggle with masturbation, here is some advice:

▶ Trust God, and ask him to work in your life. Stop trying to change your own life, and let God take control.

▶ Don't condemn yourself. Adopt God's attitude: Stop making masturbation a big deal. Ask God to help you to concern yourself more with obeying him in matters he's spoken clearly about.

▶ Control your thoughts. Avoid picturing yourself involved in immoral sex; especially avoid fantasizing about sex with someone you know. That is degrading to both you and the person.

▶ If possible, share your struggle with someone else. More than anything, this can ease the tension and guilt many feel. One girl shared her struggle with her sister, and found love, understanding, and total acceptance—which set her free from guilt and helped her quit altogether.

SECTION 4.

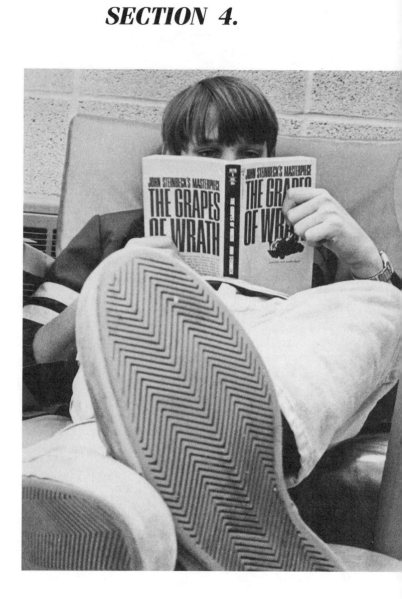

Unwrapping the Gift of Your Mind

ROHN ENGH

Your New, Improved Brain

One of the biggest challenges in high school is the academics. Much more is expected of you. High school means long-range assignments—a term paper due in October, a math assignment finished by Friday—rather than homework completed each night for the following day.

High school means taking responsibility for your own work. A junior high teacher might have hounded you for that overdue book report, but in high school you're on your own. No book report—no grade.

You're also more responsible for how you use your mind outside of class—what you feed it through the magazines and books you read (or don't read), the movies you watch, the television shows you choose, the music you listen to. While Mom and Dad may still try to exert some influence on your choices, they're aware that more and more, the choices are yours.

At twelve you weren't mentally able to handle all this responsibility; now you are. Your brain actually goes through a transformation during adolescence, and you really are capable of handling trigonometry and chemistry and the imagery in Shakespeare (though any one of these may not be your particular area of strength). Think for a second of your mind as a computer. A couple of years ago, this computer was rather primitive. It operated under the old principle "Garbage in, garbage out." You basically spit out whatever input your teachers, parents, and others gave you.

But now your brain is capable of mixing and matching, making new and more sophisticated connections with the data you've stored there. You can think analytically. Puns make sense to you now; you can discern shades of irony and sarcasm. Input is still important—perhaps more so, because of the possibility that one new piece of information can change how you think about many other things. But now you're capable of doing something new with what you learn.

And this capability will be strengthened and tested, most of all in your classes. You'll be expected to participate in class, to add your unique perspective. You'll have the opportunity to express what you think and feel in compositions and essay questions. Math and science will stretch your new-found analytical abilities. You may even find your faith challenged as you bump up against new ideas that seem contradictory to what you've always believed.

You'll need some practical skills to handle all these new challenges—not to mention the juggling act necessary to keep up a social life and take advantage of the extracurricular opportunities that are available in high school. And that's what this book is all about, so read on.

Cracking the Books and Making the Grade

You've probably heard other students say things like: "Hey, I plan to build houses, so why should I care about studying history and algebra?" Or, "You learn more by getting out and living life than you do by sitting in a classroom listening to other people talk."

Certainly there is some truth to their statements. Learning does happen apart from books and classes and school. And not every course you take is going to directly relate to whatever you end up doing. But the fact is, God has placed you in a books-and-education situation for now, and you need to learn how to cope.

Aren't there other reasons for studying, though? Maybe more practical ones? Yes—take your pick from these:

▶ Study because you have the basic ability to do the work. Nearly everyone has the skills. But a lot of students don't want to work or simply don't know how to study.

▶ Study because the habit of working hard is a good one to get into. There are plenty of things you'll be asked to do in the "real world" that won't be just-for-fun. Learning to work hard now, even when you don't feel like it, will benefit you in the coming years.

▶ Study so you'll be independent and freer once you're out of school. Educated people generally have a lot more opportunities available to them. And they learn to think for themselves, and to function in the world. Ignorance limits our lives.

▶ Study because God wants you to do your work well. He doesn't expect perfection, only that you maintain a good attitude, be prepared, and do your best. He'll handle the results.

Beware of These Sabotages to Academic Success

▶ Being unprepared or unorganized.
▶ Taking poor notes, or no notes at all.
▶ Not giving each class regular attention.
▶ Not turning in all assigned homework.
▶ Waiting so long to do projects and papers that the work becomes overwhelming.
▶ Turning in projects or homework late.
▶ Not doing extra-credit work when you have the chance.
▶ Refusing to ask for help.
▶ Not learning how to take exams.
▶ Cheating.

How to Study

Maybe your attitude toward school is good, and you work hard, but you just don't know how to study.

Then sort through these tips, and put their ideas to work for you.

▶ Start to study soon after you get home from school. Waiting to do homework at night is a habit that should be broken, because favorite TV shows come on and friends call.

▶ After each class, recopy your notes. This will help you organize your notes and familiarize yourself with the material, as well as make preparation for the test easier.

▶ Designate one hat as your "Study Hat" and one lamp as your "Study Lamp." Promise yourself that as long as this hat and lamp are on, you'll focus only on homework. Keep a second lamp at your desk for doing other work.

▶ Put bits of information on index cards or Post-it notes, then tape them in places where you'll frequently see them, such as your mirror at home or inside your locker door.

▶ Read over your notes every couple of days in your spare moments. By the time the test comes around, you'll be reviewing instead of trying to memorize the material for the first time.

▶ Teach the material to someone else. Actually say it aloud to your stuffed animals, yourself in the mirror, a friend, or your family. Don't just think; recite the information out loud.

▶ For a break in your routine, find an unusual place to study. Try sitting on top of your desk or dresser, for example.

▶ Put study material to music. Replace the words of a familiar song with facts from your notes, then sing it.

▶ Associate words or phrases with emotions by either crying or laughing while reading them.

▶ Record lectures or repeat important facts into a cassette recorder for times when you can't get to your textbook, like when you're getting ready for school, or jogging.

Foreign Language/Vocabulary

▶ When learning new words, group related words in sets of five or so, then study them one cluster at a time.

▶ For difficult words, use as many of your senses as you can. Write while looking at a word and saying it. Think about its parts and meaning. Write the word again while saying it, but without looking, then check to see if you got it right.

▶ Look for a way to relate words to something familiar, and think of this relationship as you review.

▶ Quiz yourself. To do this, fold a sheet of lined paper lengthwise. Now unfold it and put each word on one side of the fold and, on the same line, either its short definition (for English vocabulary words) or its foreign name on the other side. Finally, fold the paper in half again and pick a side, then go down the list and say the answers out loud.

Note-taking

▶ Determine the teacher's purpose. Take notes if:
—you'll need the information for a test or use in a paper. This is particularly true if your teacher is supplementing the assigned reading with more infor-

mation, or explaining difficult concepts mentioned in the book.

—the teacher gives you an assignment or explains a procedure that you'll have to do.

▶ Don't take notes if he is demonstrating a key idea that you won't have to duplicate. But listen closely.

▶ Write down key words or phrases only. Don't even try to copy things word for word. Use abbreviations and symbols when possible.

▶ Read the assignment before coming to class. That way you won't waste time taking notes on material that's already in the book.

▶ At the end of class, briefly summarize the lecture in a few sentences, answering the question, "What main points were covered today?" If you have time, do this immediately after class. If not, then do it when you get home.

Class Participation

▶ Do ask questions.

▶ If you come to class having done the assignment, you won't be as afraid to participate.

▶ Rehearse what you want to say before you say it.

Reading Books

▶ Move your index finger along the line you are reading until you feel yourself gliding through the material. This will increase your reading speed.

► Survey the entire book. Quickly flip through to see where the writer is going. Note chapter titles and subtitles, and look over the preface and conclusion.

► Read for main ideas first, and mark them. Underline or highlight key statements or place check marks by the significant points. Write notes in the margins; rephrase the author's statements. Then compile your notes by summarizing each chapter with a few brief, written comments.

► Ask questions of the author as you go, then read for his answers. Find out what the titles mean. Check diagrams and charts. Note each chapter's concluding remarks. Ask: What's the point of this section?

Speeches

► Decide on one or two major points. Then consider how you and your classmates differ in attitude, interests and knowledge of the topic. Speak in terms of their language.

► Don't read your speech, except for possibly a few carefully chosen examples that you know will work well. Brief notes on index cards will keep you organized.

► Speak to one person at a time to keep you natural. No longer than is comfortable, though (probably ten seconds or less).

► Take it slow. Your goal is to help the audience understand the topic, not to present the information in record time. Slow down, pause, and guide the audience through your talk.

► Speak the way you talk when in casual conversation with someone you respect.

► Ask for advice and criticism to make sure you aren't doing anything that distracts a listener.

Short-answer Tests

► Don't leave anything blank (unless a teacher penalizes for guessing). You may get at least partial credit for a partially right answer. You get nothing if you don't answer.

► Do what's asked. If a question is worth five points, and you remember everything the teacher said about the topic, resist the urge to write an entire page on the subject. Just cover the main points and move on.

► Pay attention to whether a later question answers a previous one. For example, question number three on a history test reads: "At the outset of the Vietnam War, the president of the United States was _____." But if question number fifteen reads: "During the early days of the Vietnam War, President Kennedy's Secretary of State was _____," you'll know the answer to question three is "John Kennedy."

Multiple Choice Tests

► Anticipate the correct answer before you read the choices.

► Eliminate all other choices by finding a good reason why each is incorrect. (If you must guess, discard the answers that are definitely wrong, and probably the extremes. The correct answer is often between two extremes.)

▶ Notice if one of the answers is longer, is stated in different vocabulary or is slightly different from the others—all clues that this may be the right answer.

▶ Reread the question and mark the correct answer.

Writing Papers

▶ Once you've chosen your subject, read about it in a general source, such as an encyclopedia (if research is necessary), and start taking notes. This will help you pinpoint the major themes to cover, as well as familiarize you with your topic.

▶ As you read, look for ideas or phrases that make you ask why or how they are true. They'll probably end up as your focal points in the paper.

▶ Before you write your first draft, come up with a thesis that states your opinion or conclusion in a simple sentence or two. Every point of your paper will need to relate to or help prove this opening.

▶ Organize your notes into a brief outline showing all the major points you want to discuss and the order in which you'll discuss them. Fit the minor points in as you go.

▶ Compile notes on index cards as you read. Write in the upper right-hand corner of each the book title and page number you're taking the information from. In the upper left-hand corner, assign this card a section that corresponds to the appropriate point on your outline, then file it.

▶ Write the first draft, but don't worry yet about grammar, spelling, style or "formal" wording. Just get your ideas on paper, using simple words and sentences.

► Once you've written this draft, leave it alone. After a few days, pull it out again and read it through, making notes of what should be changed or added. Then revise it, using more appropriate (though not necessarily bigger) words and proper English.

► Have another person read it over and make suggestions.

► Rewrite it again.

Choosing a Track

Something different about high school is that you'll get to choose a "track" or direction by picking some of your courses. If your plans involve college, you'll take a different track than if you are going into the family business immediately after graduation. Just be sure to tell your counselor your goals so you can pick classes that will put you in the right direction. And pay special attention to prerequisite courses—ones you must pass before you're allowed to take a higher-level class. You don't want to be told as a senior that you can't be in college-required World Literature because you didn't take Advanced English as a sophomore.

Your guidance counselor, a trusted teacher and your parents can help you make these decisions. Just talk to them.

Your Faith in the Classroom

Maybe you've been told that teachers in high school are always putting down Christians. Maybe you've heard that students are being forced to believe stuff like evolution, abortion rights, homosexuality and atheism. Rest assured, the rumors are greatly exaggerated. For the most part, high school teachers are simply that—teachers. They are there to teach you—to offer information that will prepare you for the next step in your studies.

As you think about your new teachers, consider the following:

▶ Teachers aren't simply teaching what they want to teach. The local school board and other official groups establish certain academic guidelines. If your teachers are going to continue teaching, they must abide by those guidelines.

▶ Teachers are concerned with your education. Contrary to what some people think, teachers generally don't spend their time plotting how to attack the Christians in their classroom. Their chief concern is your education.

▶ Teachers are people too. Like all of us, teachers have their beliefs, biases, and opinions on a variety of subjects, including religion. They also make mistakes and aren't always as fair as you'd like them to be. By realizing their biases and their human shortcomings, you can more easily forgive them when they say or do things that go against your beliefs or values.

Classroom Do's and Don'ts

When you feel your beliefs are challenged:

▶ Don't over-react or jump to conclusions. Let's say a teacher says something that puts you on the defensive or makes you angry. Give yourself time to think through the teacher's comments before you respond. You may discover that the remarks don't necessarily contradict what you believe. If you're not sure, research the topic discussed or talk to a trusted Christian adult about the teacher's perspectives.

▶ Don't challenge in front of the class. If a teacher's remarks about religion or moral values constantly "rub you the wrong way," don't make it a class debate. He will respect your concerns a lot more if you talk to him privately after class.

▶ Do be willing to answer test questions that contradict what you believe. Learning something isn't the same as believing something. You are not going against your faith by giving "required answers." You are simply demonstrating that you have learned what's been taught. For instance: Begin a biology essay on evolution by stating, "According to the textbook, evolutionists believe. . . ." In doing so, you are simply demonstrating you know the assigned material. You are not conceding that you believe it.

► Do offer your Christian perspective when appropriate. When the assignment allows, give book reports on "Christian" novels, write essays on the influence of Christianity on culture, give speeches on issues of concern to Christians. In doing so, you can offer well-researched perspectives in an appropriate and acceptable way.

► Do know both sides of the argument. Study Christian perspectives on controversial classroom issues like evolution, abortion and mercy killing (euthanasia). Along with enhancing your own understanding and knowledge, you may also discover that Christians don't always agree on every aspect of these controversial issues. If you can't find resource material, ask for help from your pastor, youth leader or the resource librarian at a local Christian school or college.

► Do stand up for what's important. While this may mean occasionally speaking out for truth, it also means simply living out what you believe. Handing homework in on time, doing your assignments the best you can, being polite in class, showing respect for the opinions of your teachers and fellow students, being honest and never cheating—all these actions communicate much more than your best arguments. They communicate that your faith is real and alive.

Perspective on Grades

Just how important are grades? Sometimes your GPA can seem like the most important thing in the world. There's all this pressure to get the very best grades—and sometimes it seems like no one is willing to settle for anything less than an A in everything. The question is, should you settle for anything less? Will getting a C- in a class forever ruin your chances of getting into a good college, getting a good job and having a good life?

Probably not. Oh, no doubt about it, a good education is important. Not just to get good jobs, either. But to learn how to think, how to get on in the world. To learn about how the world works.

And that's where grades reach their own limitation. Getting a good education and getting good grades are not necessarily one and the same thing. You can learn a great deal in school, and still get nearly average grades. And, of course, you can "cram" for a test, get an A, and forget the material in a week.

Grades are a not-completely-accurate measure of your performance in certain areas. They are somewhat dependent on how well your learning style meshes with your teachers' teaching styles (for instance, your teacher uses stories a lot, and you're easily able to remember what you hear in story form), what your aptitude is for a particular subject matter (you've always done well in math, but dreaded English), and your own personal mastery of the study skills necessary for academic success (note-taking, understanding what you read, ability to take tests, etc.).

Why Grades Are Important

Your grades don't tell everything about you. But they can be pretty important, depending on your long-term goals—which you may or may not know now. College and a career may seem a long way off to you now. And it's OK not to know what you want now. You do have time.

But consider this: In high school, you can either open up or close off options for your future. You may not know what you want to do, career-wise, but you probably have some idea of what you don't want to do. For instance, you may know that you don't want to be a trash collector all your life. Or a lifeguard. If that's the case, then you need at least to get your high-school diploma. There aren't many jobs out there that don't require at least a high-school education.

To take it a step further: You may not know for sure whether you want to be a journalist, a doctor or a missionary, but if you think these choices might interest you, it's clear that you will need at least a college education. Better take college preparatory classes and try to get the best grades you can.

The point is to keep as many options open for yourself at this time so you will have time to figure out what you really want to do, career-wise. And usually, that means getting the best grades you can without becoming obsessed by your GPA.

How to Keep Sane about Grades

▶ Do your best, and don't worry too much about the grades. Make it your goal to learn, not to get an A. The difference is the pressure you put on yourself. If you really learn the material, you'll do well. If you're uptight about getting an A, the pressure you put on yourself could interfere with your performance, even if you know the material. Performance pressure can actually block your memory.

One student, who always did very well in school, says her secret was to get involved in the material, do her best and leave the results to God. She never worried about tests, and usually did well on them because she never pressured herself. And, of course, her success just gave her confidence that she could continue to do well.

▶ Make learning into a game. Good teachers know how to do this for you. If you're lucky enough to have such a teacher, try to figure out what he or she does to make learning fun. Then see if you can transfer that to your other classes.

Diane never liked history because it always seemed like just a bunch of dates to memorize. Her ninth grade history teacher made it interesting by teaching history in story form, and relating it to current problems and events. Diane found that she learned best through story form, and whenever she could with other classes, she'd try to find out what the story was.

Her grades in history and related courses improved from then on.

▶ Try to learn about yourself as you go—and build on your strengths. In discovering that she had an interest in stories, Diane realized that English and writing were her main strengths. Later, when in college the time came to declare her major, it wasn't difficult.

▶ Learn from your mistakes as well as your successes. Getting a C doesn't have to be the end of the world. When Gary got a C- on an English paper, he felt crushed. He had always gotten A's or a B+ on his papers! Gary talked over his grade with the teacher. His teacher pointed out what Gary had missed in the book that was the subject of his report. Gary reread the book and got a lot more out of it. Though the C- still smarts, Gary will tell you that he learned a lot about how to read a book from that "failure."

▶ Don't label yourself according to your grades. Remember, grades measure your performance, not your value as a person—or even your intelligence. (It's a fact that intelligent people don't necessarily get good grades in school.) Even if you get all A's, it doesn't mean you're any better a person than someone who gets C's and D's.

Besides, grades measure only academic-type skills: how well you can absorb information through lectures, labs or reading, how well you write, how well you can take tests. To some extent, grades also measure self-discipline and motivation. But they rarely touch your aptitude when it comes to interpersonal skills, or the ability to think up new ideas, or to problem-solve in real-life situations, or to take initiative. These are very important skills for success in life.

▶ Develop other, non-academic interests to add balance to your life. Sports, extra-curricular activities (photography club, the debate team, choir or band, etc.), and church activities can add balance to your life, provide new friends, and help you learn more about yourself and your strengths. All of which can help you keep a sane perspective on grades. Better to get a B in several courses and lead a well-rounded life than to ace everything and have no other interests. Even college admissions boards will tell you that extracurricular activities are important. Really.

▶ Bring God into the picture. Ask him to help you to make the most out of school. Pray for him to help you learn, make every effort to do your best, and then leave the results with him. He cares about how you use your mind; he cares about your future. You can count on his help.

UNWRAPPING THE GIFT OF YOUR MIND 137

Movies, Music, Magazines, and Books

By the time Sean started high school, movies and videos had become his life. He couldn't see enough of them. And since he looked much older than his age, he had no trouble getting into the latest R-rated picture. Even though he came from a Christian family, he saw nothing wrong with his viewing habits. After all, he said, it's only entertainment.

Then the problems came. It seemed like he and his father were always fighting—mostly over Sean's trips to the movies. He realized he was trying to escape from his problems at home through spending more and more time at the movies. Sean also started realizing that movies were giving him some pretty warped perspectives about sex and violence. Sean finally had to admit it: Movies were more than mere entertainment. They were filled with ideas and values that were affecting his life in many bad ways. They had become an obsession.

Sean made a decision: No more movies. Like a person recovering from an addiction, Sean felt "total withdrawal" was essential. It would give him a chance to rethink and straighten out his own personal values. Eventually, Sean did start going to see movies again, but he became a lot pickier. "I read reviews. I think through what the message is, why I want to see a particular film, what it will do for (and to) me."

Sean's situation was extreme. Yet Sean's story does point out a common problem: Most of us spend little time thinking through the entertainment we see, read and listen to. Like Sean, we often think movies, TV, music, and other means of entertainment are harmless diversions—simply "fun things to do." Yet they are packed with values and perspectives that can, as Sean discovered, do us more harm than good. It really is a personal choice. Choose wisely.

Entertainment: Five Steps to Better Choices

Music? Movies? TV? Magazines? Books? How do you decide what's good and what's bad? Consider this five-point checklist:

▶ What is the message? In some cases it's easy to find the message. Certain movies make poignant and moral statements against war. Some books aptly proclaim the importance of friendship. Some rock music rightly rails against environmental pollution. Yet entertainment often carries other messages that aren't always so worthwhile or easy to recognize. Ask yourself: When a movie shows high-school students having sex together, what "message" is it giving about sex? When a rock song praises partying, what "message" is it giving about alcohol and drugs? When a horror video shows a madman hacking up teenagers, what "message" is it giving about the value of human life?

▶ Is it exploitative? First, let's consider what's not exploitative. Take classroom classics like *All's Quiet on the Western Front, Lord of the Flies,* and *The Red Badge of*

Courage. All three contain rather graphic depictions of violence. But that doesn't mean they exploit violence. As a matter of fact, all three novels demonstrate the horribleness and immorality of violent actions. On the other hand, books and movies that depict plenty of gore and blood "just for the fun of it," that glorify war and killing, that never show the human pain of death, are pure exploitation. They use and misuse violence simply to increase box office and book sales. Music videos that are sexually graphic and pornographic magazines like *Playboy* are also exploitative.

Here's a good rule to guide you: If movies, books, or magazines depict men or women in demeaning ways, if they glorify human cruelty, if they never show the consequences of immoral or violent behavior, if they appeal purely to our lusts or our own tendency toward violence—they're exploitative.

▶ What's on your mind? When you turn off your favorite sitcom or when you walk out of the theater, what's going through your head? Are you thinking about some thought-provoking message? Are you thinking about a funny scene that gave you a good, healthy laugh? On the other hand, is your mind doing a rerun of the movie's graphic depiction of sex or violence? Or are you feeling like acting as rude as one of the sitcom's characters? A TV show, movie, or book may be considered great entertainment; it may even offer a good message here and there. Yet if it leaves you thinking garbage, then consider it worthy of the trash—and not your mind.

▶ Is this reality? There's nothing wrong with escaping into a good flick now and then. Yet if we start believing what we see on TV and at the movies, we are accepting fantasy over fact. Here are a few of the more harmful Hollywood fantasies: To be considered beautiful, a girl must look like a model. Couples who date each other should eventually sleep together. People who are worth anything must wear great clothes, live in big houses and drive fancy cars. Those aren't just fantasies—they're lies.

▶ Is this "smart" entertainment? Film critic Roger Ebert once told *Campus Life* magazine: "Don't see movies that are dumber than you are." Good advice. Does a movie or TV show insult your intelligence? Then don't insult yourself by watching it.

Christian Entertainment Only?

Christian entertainment only may be the best decision for you right now, particularly if you're a new Christian. You may need time to absorb the distinctly Christian view of life, so that some questionable idea doesn't sway you from a faith you don't yet fully understand.

With that said, we must be careful about putting down others for enjoying entertainment that isn't labeled "Christian." God has given all kinds of people—Christians and non-Christians—incredible gifts of creativity. Sculptors create beautiful statues. Composers write wonderful pieces of music. Do their works of art have value only if they scrawl "Jesus" on them? Or is there a place in art to celebrate God's good gifts of love and friendship and nature? And isn't there a place for media like film to speak against injustice? And isn't there a place in music simply to reflect the joy of a melody?

To say Christians should never enjoy secular entertainment (providing its values don't contradict God's values) is somewhat like saying we shouldn't enjoy a good swim, a walk in the park, or a purple sunset. God's creations and those things that God allows us to create are to be enjoyed. With thanksgiving.

AS THE YOUNG TADPOLE DEVELOPS, IT BEGINS TO FEED ON DECAYING TWIGS AND LEAVES.

WHEN NORM ASKED LOLA TO SEE A MOVIE SHE DIDN'T THINK HE MEANT THE THIRD PERIOD BIOLOGY MOVIE ON POND LIFE.

Reading for Entertainment

As you enter high school, you will discover that reading lists get longer and longer. You may even come to think of reading as merely something teachers assign. Yet it's much more than that. As the old saying goes, "The book really is better than the movie!"

Why? Because good writing always makes the "picture in your head" better than the picture on a movie screen. No amount of special effects and no amount of dramatic acting can ever outdo a great novel teamed with your imagination. So instead of popping another tape in the VCR, instead of vegging out in front of another boring sitcom, open a great book for a good change.

Need some suggested reading? Ask your English teacher and school librarian for a list of popular novels. (Tell them the type of book you like best: science fiction, fantasy, contemporary, historical.) Also, *Campus Life* magazine's "Expressions" column highlights current reads worth checking out.

Go ahead, read a book. It really is great entertainment.

Managing Your Time

Campus Life magazine recently surveyed its high-school readers, and here are some of the findings: about 50 percent have a job, 66 percent are involved in sports, almost 50 percent are active in music, 47 percent are members of student organizations, and over 90 percent spend an hour or more each week on church-related activities.

The thought of such "busy-ness" can be pretty overwhelming. You start to wonder: Will there be time in high school for everything? Will I even have time to eat and sleep?

Most high schoolers would tell you that yes, there's time for being involved, having friends and doing homework. You just have to use your time wisely.

As a matter of fact, high school will help you learn the fine art of budgeting your time: doing what must be done, and still having time for the things you want to do.

First, though, let's look at one of the biggest time-management struggles for high-school students.

WELCOME TO HIGH SCHOOL

Procrastination

Sound familiar? For many, many students, the biggest struggle is procrastination, putting off the things you should do.

You're probably a procrastinator if:

▶ You're afraid to fail.

▶ You have very high expectations of yourself.

▶ You either wait until the last minute to start projects, or take twice as long as most people to finish them (because you want your work to be perfect).

It's a common problem in school, but it is also a problem that affects other areas of your life, such as cleaning your room or keeping a journal.

Here's some help for moving out of procrastination:

▶ Make a list of projects to be done.

▶ Pray for God's help and insight as to which project you should tackle first.

▶ Break down big projects into several smaller ones.

▶ Do one activity at a time.

▶ Remove any distractions.

▶ Allow more time than you think is needed.

▶ Begin the day with the most difficult, least enjoyable, or most urgent project.

▶ Mark through each task as you finish, and then reward yourself for it.

▶ Make a "backup list" of projects—things you mean to do when you have time—and use them as part of your reward system.

Avoiding Burnout

You may be thinking, I don't put things off. . . . I just don't know how I'm going to handle everything! It's true that high school offers a greater variety of choices than you had in junior high—more sports, music organizations, clubs, service groups, and classes. With some careful thought, you can manage the demands and still maintain your balance.

▶ Love it or leave it. Decide what your goals and priorities are first, and with those in mind, say yes only to the opportunities that matter—the things you love to do.

▶ Do your "homework." Before joining a new organization or taking on a new responsibility, talk about what it requires with people who are already involved. And watch them to see how much time the activity demands.

▶ Just say "No way." Other people are capable and willing to get involved, so say no when the activity doesn't seem to "fit" you.

▶ Pass it on. Delegate when you can. Accomplish by teamwork rather than independently.

▶ Organization is a must. Keep a calendar with meetings, events, homework deadlines, performances, games, and nights out with friends so you'll know how to plan your time each week.

▶ I need my space! Purposely schedule regular blocks of free time that will give you room to breathe.

▶ Make room for God. Having a quiet time with God each day helps you relax, and will get your mind off of your things-to-do-today list.

▶ Don't forget your friends and family. The people who care about you play a big role in preventing burnout. They're a source of renewal when you're worn out, encouragement when you fail, support when you're discouraged and laughter when you're in a bad mood. So make sure you take time to be with them.

▶ Tell me my limits. Ask trusted peers and adults to help you set limits. Give them permission to tell you if they see you're doing too much or are stressed out.

AN EXTREME CASE OF POST-EXAM BURNOUT.

SECTION 5.

Making God Your Best Friend

LUKE GOLOBITSH

Help for Our Deepest Needs

Most of us can't get enough of friendship. We crave having someone who deeply understands us; who is always there to listen; who will forgive us when we've wronged them; who will help us make good decisions; someone we can laugh and cry with, whom we can talk to about anything in the world; someone who will stick by us when we hit rough times.

Some of us are fortunate enough to find one or two such friends in a lifetime. But eventually we discover that even the best of friendships is flawed in some way. No one is always available, always giving, always willing to listen, always faithful, always forgiving, always perfectly loving. Yet we're built to want that kind of love and faithfulness and companionship.

The Bible has some good news on this front: Someone can satisfy our craving. Jesus Christ became human specifically to understand firsthand what it's like to be human and tempted (Hebrews 2:18), and to restore the relationship with our Father in heaven that was broken by our rebellion from God. He did this by personally bearing in our place the penalty for that rebellion—death (Hebrews 2:14–15, 5:8–9). Jesus promises those who receive him and accept his sacrifice that he will be the Ultimate Friend: "Surely I am with you always, even to the end of the age. Never will I leave you; never will I forsake you" (Matthew 28:20; Hebrews 13:5).

Imagine: Friendship with God is available, free! No fees to pay, no conditions to meet. Just someone who is always there, who always cares, who is both able and willing to help you at any time. Someone who truly forgives and forgets (see Psalm 103:8–14).

Such a Friend is deeply interested in your high-school experience. He wants you to succeed, not just in the superficial ways like making good grades and good friends, but in the deeper ways. He's interested in the kind of person you become. He is more than willing to be involved in every aspect of your life, if you let him.

And how do you let him? Well, by getting to know him more and more as Friend.

Think about how you get close to a friend: You spend time together; you talk about all kinds of concerns; you come to rely on your friend, trusting in the person's faithfulness to you. You talk about your friend with others (in positive terms of course). And you want to do things for your friend to express your appreciation.

Cultivating a friendship with God is not too different. Spending time with him, reading his word to you (the Bible) and talking to him (prayer) helps you get to know him better. You find out some of his promises, rely on them and find them to be true. You want to be around others who also appreciate his friendship. You talk about him with others. And, as you get to know him as Faithful Friend, you look for opportunities to do good things for him—which, Jesus told us, was best accomplished by looking for ways to meet human needs.

As you get to know God as friend, you'll find something interesting happening: You become more like him. But when you think about it, that's pretty natural. Don't you generally become more like the people you hang around with?

So there's a bonus if you become friends with God. Not only do you discover a fabulous Friend who will never let you down, but you also gain the potential of becoming a super friend to others. You're getting to know the person who invented friendship, after all.

Getting to Know God

No friendship survives without spending time together. Lots of time. Your closest friends are those with whom you spend the most time and share the most personal thoughts and feelings.

So it makes sense that in order to have a friendship with God, you have to spend time with him. But how do you do that? If he's always with you anyway, is there any real need to set aside special time? And how do you "spend time with" someone you can't even see or touch?

There are two keys to spending time with God and cultivating a relationship that will feel real to you: the Bible, and faith.

The Bible is God's Book, his record of what he's like. It tells what he wants you to know about him and how he works. It suggests how to have a relationship with him. The Bible, God's Word, gets you in touch with his presence. Think of it as a collection of letters from a good friend. When you receive a letter from a close friend, can't you just hear the person's voice behind the words? Don't you get a sense of his presence as you read the letter?

In order to connect with God and his Word to you, you need a little faith. Not a whole lot—Jesus said that faith the size of the tiniest seed is enough. And what is faith? Hebrews 11:1 says, "It is the confident assurance that something we want is going to happen. It is the certainty that what we hope for is waiting for us, even though we cannot see it up ahead." And verse 6 says, "You can never please God without faith, without depending on him. Anyone who wants to come to God must believe that there is a God and that he rewards those who sincerely look for him" (The Living Bible).

So faith is believing that what you read in God's Word is true, and trying your best to obey it. It's believing that God is with you, that he can help you with your problems. It's believing that when you talk to him, he hears you and will grant you your request— or gently refuse it because he has something better in mind.

By faith, you realize that the God who created an immense universe, complete with galaxies huge beyond the imagination of human beings, the One who knows everything that ever happened and ever will happen— this God longs to spend time with you! (Check out Revelation 3:20.) You trust that when you set aside a few minutes each day to read God's Book and to talk to him, you really are spending time with him and getting to know him as Ultimate Friend.

How to Spend Time with God

OK, so you've decided spending time with God is a good idea. How do you go about doing it? Here are some suggestions:

▶ Decide on a regular time and place. This is not meant to be a straitjacket, but a set time and place ensures the meeting will happen. Most people find either the morning, the time right after school or supper, or the time before bed to work best. It should be a time when you can be alone, without interruptions, and when you're fairly alert mentally. Many call this appointment "quiet time," which is an apt description of what you're trying to do: get quiet and focus on God for twenty or thirty minutes a day.

▶ Use a good, clear Bible translation that you like. Make sure it's a modern translation that is easy for you to understand. Many find the *NIV Student Bible* or the *Youth Application Bible* (*Living Bible*) helpful. Both of these Bible editions include a plan for reading through the Bible in a set period of time (the *NIV Student Bible* has three separate reading tracks).

You might also use a devotional guide, which typically presents a passage of Scripture, includes a short writing about the passage, and may suggest a memory verse and/or topic for prayer. There are many such devotionals available. Two that teenagers have particularly found helpful are *Alive* and *Alive 2*, both by S. Rickly Christian.

▶ Before you begin reading, pray that God will help make his Word real to you. Read expectantly. Ask yourself about each passage:

—Is there a promise for me to claim?

—Is there a command for me to obey?

—Is there a warning for me to listen to?

—Does this passage point out a sin I need to confess?

—Is there something here about God that I can praise him for, or trust him about, or thank him for?

▶ Use a notebook to write things down. Write down what you discovered, whether it's a promise, a warning, a command, etc. Also jot down how you think God wants you to respond. Remember, your quiet time notebook is just between you and God. He's not going to correct your spelling or punctuation.

▶ Talk back to God about what you've read. Prayer is just as important as reading. It's the time when you get to respond to God. Talk to him about what you've read. Ask him to give you the strength to obey. Praise him; thank him for becoming real to you. Confess your sin.

And of course, it's perfectly fine—in fact, it's very important—for you to talk to God about your problems. He wants to help you in every area of your life. "Cast all your anxiety on him because he cares for you" says 1 Peter 5:7. Whether it's a test you're preparing for, a relationship you're trying to work out, a temptation you're facing, a depression you're working through—God cares, and he wants to help. Ask him for help, and trust that he will answer.

It's a good idea to write these prayers and concerns down in your quiet time notebook. That way you can look back over your notebook and see ways God has worked in your life: what you've learned about him and how that's changed your life, and how he has helped you with that test or relationship or temptation or depression.

▶ Use your imagination to help the Bible come alive. When reading a story or a psalm, for instance, try to picture what was happening or how the writer was feeling. Imagine God is next to you, describing how he feels about you or how he'd like you to live. When you pray, imagine yourself handing your problem over to Jesus in a paper bag, or laying that ugly sin at the foot of the cross, and leaving it there. God gave you your imagination, and it can be used in positive ways.

▶ Take note of especially meaningful verses. When a verse or passage seems to leap out of your Bible at you, take time to really reflect on it. Or you may even want to memorize it. Write it down in your notebook, say it aloud several times, and repeat it to yourself often. Some people write verses down on index cards and carry them in their wallet or purse, so they can refer to them periodically throughout the day.

Maybe Bible memorization reminds you of dull Sunday school classes. But the impact on your life can be far from dull. Dave says he is grateful that he memorized Psalm 23 way back in third grade. "I have remembered that psalm since then in discouraging times, and it comforts me."

Todd, a junior in high school, says that he's glad

for the verses he'd been "forced" to memorize. "Now I really see how those verses apply to my life in many ways." For instance, when he was tempted by sex, he remembered 1 Corinthians 10:13 about temptation and God's provision of a way out. Todd sought that way out, and was kept from falling into sin and hurting himself and another person.

Talking to God during your quiet time isn't the only time to pray, of course. Bringing him into your day throughout the day is another way to get close to him.

Improving Your Talks with God

Talking to your best friend is easy. Why? Because you know him. You know what makes him happy. You know what makes him sad. And the closer you get the better you know him. So you talk. About your dreams. Your fears. Your frustrations. Your gripes. And your joys. You're close. So you talk.

Now what about talking to God? Not so easy, not so natural. Suddenly we wonder what to say and how to say it. We don't even call it talk. We call it prayer. Our tone of voice changes, our language begins to sound "holy." We make it quick. Get it over. It's "Hi God!" then "Good-bye God."

Why is talking to God so different from talking to our best friend? Obviously, we can see our friend. We can't see God. That's a big difference. And there's not much we can do about it. But there are other things we can do something about. We can get to know God better through reading his book, through spending more time with others who call him friend, through learning to enjoy and appreciate what he's done and made. As we get to know him better, we begin to learn what makes him happy, what makes him sad. When that happens, we become closer and discover: He is worthy of our trust. So we begin to talk to him, more freely and openly. About our dreams. Our fears. Our frustrations. Our gripes. And our joys. When that happens, talking to God becomes easy and natural— like talking to a best friend.

Making God-Talks a Part of Your Daily Routine

You may have heard the Bible phrase: "Pray continually" (1 Thessalonians 5:17). And you wonder: What does it mean? Consider Diane's thoughts:

"I take at least one hour every morning to shower, blow-dry my hair, dress, make my lunch, and eat breakfast. One day, a question popped into my mind: What would it take to prepare my heart as carefully as I prepare my body?

"As I reflected on the thought, I remembered a verse somewhere about 'clothing yourself with Christ.' I found it in Romans 13:14. So I began to imagine 'clothing myself with Christ' while I dressed, and I prayed that I would live that day in his strength.

"I found other Bible ideas and images that helped me combine my physical and spiritual preparations for the day. While I shower, I can confess my failures and picture them being washed away by Jesus. When I dab on perfume, I can pray that I would be the "fragrance of Christ" to those I meet that day (see 2 Corinthians 2:14–16). Fixing my hair and putting on makeup, I can pray that I will remember to smile, say a kind word to someone—that my words and presence would add a little beauty to people that day. And when I eat breakfast, I'm reminded that without God's Word, my soul will get hungry (see Luke 4:4).

"I don't always remember to pray through the morning in this way. But, when I forget for too long, the question pops into my mind: What would it take to prepare myself on the inside as carefully as I prepare myself on the outside?"

Diane obviously isn't praying non-stop, yet she is trying to see how her God-talks fit into the small routines that take up her time. You can do it too. You can sit in English class and, glancing over at a friend whose parents are divorcing, you can pray. You can join in a game of noon-time basketball and think about teamwork. Then, even while dribbling across the court, you can pray that you and your Christian friends will work together as a team. There are many ways to combine the activities of the day with the activity of prayer. As you remember to do so, you may begin to understand what it really means to "pray without ceasing."

Why We Don't Always Get What We Want

Consider this: "The Spirit helps us in our weakness. We do not know what we ought to pray, but the Spirit himself intercedes for us" (Romans 8:26).

Sometimes when we do not know what to pray, we clam up. More often we pray anyway.

At times we are positive we know what to pray. But if we had a bit more insight, we would know how little we know. We do our best, try our hardest to pray the right way. And God does want to hear our concerns, even if feebly expressed. But he is wise enough and good enough to not always give us what we ask. Why? Because what we ask might be good, but somehow it does not fit together with a lot of other good things to make a perfect plan. So we pray and God's Spirit adjusts our prayers and modifies them to fit God's will. When it comes to prayer, what more could we possibly want?

Four Things to Talk to God About

When you talk to God, say:

▶ *Thanks!* Remember to say "thank you" and also be sure to tell him how much you appreciate him. Need help? Read through Psalms 144–150.

▶ *I'm sorry!* Clear the air. Clean the slate. Say you're sorry when you've made a mistake or done something wrong.

▶ *I've got this problem* . . . Voice your concerns, your needs, your problems. God cares. He wants to hear it all.

▶ *I know this person who* . . . God cares about others—we should too. And remember: When we ask God to help someone, he may turn the prayer around and say, "Won't you go and answer it for me?"

Praying as a Team

It's good to pray alone. It's good to talk personally and openly with God. You can say things to him you'd never say in front of others. That's fine, even good. But there comes a time for teamwork.

Look at it like this: You lift weights to get yourself in shape. But when you join the football team, you're no longer just concerned about you. You care about the other players. You care about teamwork. You need the team. Sure, you continue to lift weights. But now you must also work out with the team.

It's the same with prayer. You need some team players. Guys who can help you—guys you can help. Find two or three good Christian friends who can join you regularly for group talks with God. Before school. After school. During lunch. Two or three times a week. Pick a time. Don't get too windy. Keep it short. But keep it regular. You need it. And so does your "team."

Buy God a Notebook

Buy a three-ring binder that you will use only for prayer. In this binder, list what you ask and when you ask it. You might want to separate your request into two categories: "What I Ask for Me;" "What I Ask for Others." Give a page for each category, adding new pages as needed. Leave five or six spaces between each request. In the spaces you will record your observations of God at work, how he answers yes or no.

Of course, simply listing prayers can at times seem too impersonal, too mechanical. When that happens, try brainstorming with God. Open your notebook to a blank page. In the center of the page write your concern. For example: "Mom is very sick."

Now brainstorm with God. Think about that concern from different angles. Write these new thoughts on the page, randomly, anywhere you like. As you brainstorm, get specific. For example: "When she's sick she worries about who will do her work—take care of the younger kids, cover household chores, etc." "She's fearful because her dad had cancer; she wonders if it will happen to her." "She doesn't want to worry the family."

Prayer lists and short prayers are fine. But instead of always tossing up a quick prayer or jotting down a short request, think about your concerns in detail. Look at them from different angles. Doing so will help you pray more specifically and intelligently.

Talking about My Faith

Imagine this: The summer before your first year in high school, your very best friend—let's call him Tim—moves to another state. All summer long you and Tim work hard to keep your friendship alive. You write each other constantly. You call occasionally. You even send taped messages back and forth.

Finally, it's time for school to begin and you decide it's also time to make some new friends. Not to replace Tim, of course. No new friend could do that. But you just feel kind of lonely and would like to meet some new people. So you do.

Then suddenly, two months into your freshman year, you get a call from Tim. Excitedly he tells you he's moving back. When you hang up, you can't wait for Tim to arrive. You also can't wait to tell your other friends the good news: "You know the guy Tim I've been telling you about? . . . Well, he's coming back!" When Tim finally arrives, you immediately lead him around school, introducing him to all your friends: "This is my best friend Tim! . . ."

Telling others about your Christian faith is a lot like introducing them to your best friend. But it's so much more. In fact, your relationship with Jesus is the most important friendship you'll ever have. So isn't it a friendship worth sharing with your non-Christian friends? After all, they need a Faith Friendship with Jesus, too.

When Your Faith Turns Off Your Friends

Conformity is the code of high school. When you go against that code—which, by definition, Christians do—your non-Christian friends apply pressure to make you stop. Your friends want assurance from you that certain activities are OK, like gossiping about teachers or other students, forming cliques, and partying on weekends filled with alcohol and sex.

Remember, your friends see Christianity differently than you do. To them it appears as a threat to their lifestyle. In their eyes you are not a happy young Christian; you're a once-normal person who has suddenly gone slightly weird. They hope you'll recover, but if you don't . . . too bad.

How much pressure you receive is partly up to you. The stronger you push your views on them, the stronger they'll resist. If you come on too strong, or make yourself offensive or arrogant, pressure will be applied to make you stop.

Again, try to put yourself in your friends' place. How would you feel if someone you have known for a long time came up to you one day and told you your life was a waste? And furthermore, the only way to set it right was to do exactly as he said, or else you're doomed. How would that make you feel? A bit defensive? Hostile?

So go easy on people around you. Explosive

witnessing and bold challenges to their lifestyles may not be the best plan of action around your non-Christian friends. They are reached better by your kind words and good example. If what you have is worth getting close to, they will see that in you. And if they want it, they'll soon be asking you about it.

What to Say about Your Faith

Here are four important points to cover when talking to someone about their need for a Faith Friendship with Jesus.

► God cares about you. God not only loves you—he likes you. He thinks you're valuable and important. He wants to know you and wants to be your Faith Friend. (See Matthew 9:36; John 3:16; John 15:13; 1 John 3:16, 4:16.)

► But there's a problem between you and God. Let's put it this way—all of us have this natural-born tendency to do wrong. True, we may not always act on this tendency. But it is always there. And no matter how much we try to do good, and no matter how much good we do, that tendency to do wrong remains constant. Always tempting us. Always trying to pull us in a bad direction. You could call it a "bad disposition" or a lousy "character flaw." God's Book calls it "sin." We're all born with it. We can't get rid of it. And because we have it, we are separated from God. God's goodness keeps him from being able to even get close to any badness. As a result, we will remain, even after death, separated from a Faith Friendship with God. Some people refer to this separation as a very big "gap" or "chasm." There is no way we can cross it. We are trapped on the other side—away from God. And that's very bad news. (See Romans 3:10–12, 23; Ephesians 2:1–3; Isaiah 64:6.)

▶ God offers a solution. Now some very good news. God came to Earth—in the form of a human named Jesus—and put a bridge over the gap. He did the gap-bridging—not us. How? Since Jesus was God's Special Son (or God come as man) he came to earth with no badness in him. But when he was murdered by Roman crucifixion, he pulled all of humanity's badness into him. So when he died physically, he also died spiritually. That is, he was literally separated from God because of our (and everybody else's) badness. As strange and mysterious as it may sound, he took our place. He died for our badness so we would not have to go on being separated from God.

But here's the important part: Jesus proved his power over death by coming back to life. Because Jesus rose again, each one of us can know God intimately forever—even after physical death. (See John 1:29; Ephesians 2:8–9; Romans 5:6–8; John 14:6; 2 Corinthians 5:17.)

▶ We must accept God's solution. A real friend never forces his friendship on us—we must accept that gift of friendship. It is the same with a Faith Friendship with God. Each of us must make our own personal decision to accept it. We cannot do anything good enough to begin our Faith Friendship. We can only choose to take it as a free gift God offers us. It's a decision we make through a faith talk with God. For instance: "God, I know I have this tendency to do wrong, this deep badness in me. Please forgive me and give me the ability to do what's right. Please make me a special Faith Friend of yours." The exact wording doesn't matter—what matters is that you mean and believe what you say. If you do, then God will forgive your badness and be your special Faith Friend forever. It's a promise—and like a good friend, God doesn't go back on his promises. (See Ezekiel 36:26–27; John 1:12, 3:16; Romans 10:9–10; Ephesians 2:4–9; 1 John 1:9.)

The Church: A Very Special Friendship Group

Try walking against a crowd in a jam-packed hallway. It's impossible. The crowd will either knock you down and walk over you or force you to go their way. It's the same with trying to live out our faith without Christian friends. We'll either get our faith "trampled" by the crowd or the crowd will "turn us around"—away from our beliefs.

We need friendships with Christians—especially Christians who are convinced that their Faith Friendship with Jesus is the most important friendship they have. And while these Christian friends are far from perfect, they are at least trying hard to live close to their Faith Friend. They are trying to avoid actions and attitudes that hurt their Faith Friendship. They are doing things that help their Faith Friendship get better. As you get closer to these friends, you will see good changes in your own Faith Friendship, too.

Who's a Part of Your Special Friendship Group?

Think about Christian friends and what comes to mind? Your church youth group, maybe? Or do you think about the kids in the Christian club at school?

Now think in broader, bigger terms. Think of grandmother and grandfather types, think of mother and father types, think of older brother and sister types, think of younger brother and sister types, think of aunt and uncle types. Think of all the people in your church. Each one of them is an important part of your Special Friendship Group. Together you are friends, with common beliefs, goals, and values. You are a Friendship Group that needs one another. They need your special talents, abilities, and gifts. You need their special talents, abilities, and gifts. You need the wise advice, counsel, and role modeling that older friends provide. They need the youthful enthusiasm and energy you and your friends are able to offer. Expand your view of friendship and discover what it means to be a part of your church—your Special Friendship Group.

What Does Your Special Friendship Group Offer?

Friendship gives you the opportunity to get closer to people you like to be around—who share some of your same likes and dislikes. Now think about your church: It gives you the opportunity to get closer to those who share a common Faith Friendship with Jesus.

It offers more than that, though. Your church also gives you the opportunity to get to know Jesus better. Here's how:

▶ By giving you opportunities to show your appreciation for your Faith Friendship. Imagine this: You're playing basketball and you sink one from mid-court to win the game. The team captain runs up and says, "Great shot!" His comment makes you feel pretty good. Then suddenly you're surrounded by every player on the team. They're shouting all at once: "Fantastic!" "Boy, are you good!" "Man, what a shot!" But that's not all. They lift you up on their shoulders and parade you around the gym—showing you off to everybody. You've never felt better.

Now think about church on Sunday morning. Your Special Friendship Group comes together to "lift God up on their shoulders." To say, as a group, "You're Fantastic!" Imagine how God loves this and you'll catch a glimpse of why Christians need to worship together.

▶ By cheering you on. Running a marathon is exhausting. Yet just when the runner feels like giving up, he turns into the final stretch and sees the crowd. They're yelling, cheering, shouting encouragement. Suddenly he is charged with new energy and sprints to the end. That's the way it is with our Faith Friendship. Sometimes we get tired, discouraged. Or maybe we make some mistakes or do something we shouldn't. We feel guilty and unworthy of our Faith Friendship. When that happens, our Christian friends are there, offering encouragement, direction, cheering us on— helping us to get back "in the race."

▶ By teaching you more. If your Faith Friendship with Jesus is going to get better, stronger, more mature, you need to know more about him. So jot down a note during the morning sermon, remember a key idea from Sunday school class. It's the way to grow.

▶ By helping out. Christian friends need the help of other Christian friends. Your church needs you. How? Join the choir. Teach Sunday school. Go on a summer missions trip. Be an usher. Talk to your pastor about how you can serve your Special Friendship Group.

▶ By offering you a place to belong. The church also offers small friendship groups within the larger group. So if you feel lost in the crowd, look for a small group of Christian friends who can give you the special attention you need. Maybe it's through a weekly Bible study group. Or through a group committed to community service. Or through a group that goes out to talk to others about their Faith Friendship with Jesus.

Talk to your pastor or youth leader about finding a group to meet your needs and interests.

When There Are Problems with Your Church

Unfortunately, as with any group of friends, problems do come to churches. Cliques form and you feel left out and ignored. The youth group becomes inactive and boring. Certain kids act differently at church than they do at school. Adults seem less than supportive. Whatever the problem may be, why not consider being part of the solution? Here are three steps you can take:

▶ Talk to someone. You may not feel alone in your dissatisfaction. Chances are at least a couple of other people share your feelings. If you sense someone else may struggle with the same problem, bring up the subject at an appropriate time and place. The idea is not to start a gripe session, but to express how you feel and then brainstorm some possible solutions.

▶ Pray. Even if you find only one other person who shares your desire to change things, prayer can multiply your power. Pray with the person for ideas for change. Pray that you'll be able to forgive those who may have let you down or hurt you in some way.

▶ Begin change with you. Is the youth group dwindling? Organize a retreat and invite your friends. Have the kids at your church divided into cliques? You and others who sense this problem can work harder to reach out to new people or people who might not belong to the cliques. Does it bother you that some people talk to you at youth group and not at school? Bring it up at youth group, and suggest lunchtime get-togethers once or twice a week.

The Difference God Makes

Getting to know God, and letting him make a difference in your life, is a lifelong process. So relax. Don't expect perfection overnight. Just do your best day by day to spend time with him, reading his Word and talking to him, seeking his help, trusting him with your problems, and obeying what you know to be true. Confess your sin when you fail, and ask him to help you carry on. Talk about your Friend to others when it's natural to do so, search out encouragement from others who try to live God's way—and be willing to give encouragement and help whenever you can.

None of these are big demands, really. It's the little, day-by-day decisions and choices you make that add up to a lifetime of following Jesus.

Lisa's Story

Lisa had always had a problem with peer pressure. She knew God didn't approve of her friends' idea of "party," but she just couldn't say no.

One summer she decided things had to change. She got close to people at her church, and asked God to help her be bold about her faith. At a retreat, the speaker challenged everyone to set a precedent the very first day of school and then keep it up. He gave an example: Wear a T-shirt with a Christian message, or carry a Bible. Lisa made a commitment to take a stand for Jesus right from the start.

First thing in the morning of the first day of school, her youth pastor called. "How are you going to stick by your commitment?" he asked. Lisa had a T-shirt with the words "Be Not Ashamed" on it. She said she could wear that.

But she struggled inwardly. Who wants to wear a simple T-shirt on the first day of school? But she had promised, and she wore that T-shirt.

A few people did ask her about it. Lisa gulped and said, "It means I'm not ashamed of Jesus Christ. He's the Lord of my life."

Taking that stand was the start of big changes in Lisa's life. She found Christian friends, people with whom she could be herself. They started a Bible study, invited others. Several who had asked about Lisa's T-shirt eventually became Christians and attended the Bible study.

And Lisa conquered her peer pressure problem. She tells people her relationship with Jesus is more important than partying. To her surprise, they accept her position. "I'm finding as I try to be a friend to others, and as I take a firm stand for Christ, that I actually have more and better friends than ever."

Lisa is discovering that high school with Jesus is better than she had ever hoped it could be.

WELCOME TO HIGH SCHOOL

David's Story

David became a Christian just before his freshman year of high school. He had read the Bible even before he received Jesus, but now it was more personal. When he read Luke 6:27–36 for the first time, it floored him. It's the passage about loving and doing good to your enemies, turning the other cheek, lending to other people without expecting anything in return. Within a year, David had the chance to find out firsthand how someone can follow Jesus' words.

David did well in shop. He decided to design and build a bookshelf for his mother for Christmas. The day he was to put the final touches on it, it was gone. Someone had stolen it! The shop teacher found out it had been Andy.

David, a football player and big for his age, was ready to teach Andy a lesson. But something happened when he saw Andy walk into the empty shop class that day after school. He saw the smaller boy's scared face, and the hatred just leaked out of him. Andy said, "Here's your bookshelf. I'm sorry." He set down the shelf, turned, and fled.

Later that night, as David pondered what had happened in that classroom, he remembered Jesus' words about loving your enemy. Suddenly he knew what Jesus wanted him to do.

Four days later, David asked a friend of Andy's to have Andy meet him after school. Again in an empty classroom, David and Andy confronted one another. But this time David presented Andy with an identical bookshelf. He said, "Andy, I want to give you this. It's not just a gift from me to you but also from me to

Jesus. I'd never be able to do this if it weren't for Jesus."

David didn't know what else to say. All he knew was that God had touched his life and he wanted to share it.

David walked Andy home that day, and got to know and understand him better. He invited Andy to youth group on Thursday afternoons. When there was a youth group retreat and Andy couldn't afford to go, David and his friends scraped up the money for him. And at that retreat, Andy decided to become a Christian.

David says, "Once Andy had been my enemy, but God gave me the miraculous strength to love him when I wanted to hate him. All I had done was respond to what I thought God was telling me through his Word. Now here was Andy, all excited about God.

"But at that moment," David adds, "I doubted if Andy's excitement could have matched mine." David was learning what it meant to make Jesus part of his everyday, high-school life, and was finding it a thrill.